lukelove

MY BOY
MY GRIEF
MY JOURNAL

LOSING A CHILD TO OPIOIDS

SHEILA SCOTT

1

For all our broken souls

ISBN: 9781981092390

THIS JOURNAL

Was never meant to be read, not even by myself.
It was my outlet to settle my panic and grief, to sort my mind, to explore what I was not understanding.
To log what I felt in this time when I felt so much in so many directions and sometimes felt nothing at all.
Nothing and too much.

When I was asked to write a book - I could not.
I tried.
The emotion, so raw, was merely a narrative.
And so I offer you my journal.

I offer this up to be read, not to set myself or Luke apart from those who also suffer as part of the roadkill of this opioid crisis. It is an offering of my personal experience in the hope that it may help others who may find themselves here.

This disease makes us all feel crazy.
It invokes stigma.
And helplessness.
It is threatening and dreaded by those who fear my position and Luke's.
It's a situation we all fear and in that fear we would all choose to deny its possibilities.
The insanity and loneliness that is grief.
The insanity and loneliness of substance use disorder.
The insanity of loss, so deep.

It's all here - laid bare.

I have changed the name of the boy who was with Luke on the night that he died, because, in the world of drug use, he could have been anyone.

SHOCK

Like a baby, born as nature willed, for protection of overloading the senses, buffered from what I am not ready to see, I hear that my son is dead. As I write less than 12 hours from hearing the news, I am still not hearing the news.
An elaborate dream or the passive viewing of a boring film, I have no feeling for any character.

The white noise of life, the ringing in my ears, where speech and senses once were, like the tone that is left after a loud concert or dance club and guards your senses.

The veil shades your eyes from what you can't see. The tone of white noise in your ears that shields you from what you cannot bear to hear and your brain stills your thoughts to a third-party world protecting everything that you need to grasp onto; to breathe, to live. In this all I can sense is to hold my remaining son as my soul is stretched beyond any concept of grief and in truth I feel nothing or rather, I can't feel what I know I must. The death of my firstborn child, ...what colour is that?
Traveling towards certain agony, containing a grief so vast into the confines of my tiny airline seat.

Words pass through my ears, the words of American TV, familiar and alien and now about my child.
Let this be a dream. Waiting, waiting, waiting for the horror of reality.

Warm words of loving friends wash across my senses, but I can feel nothing but the happiness that Luke evoked in these kind broken-hearted souls.

I ache to smell him, to hear the slamming of doors, the booming
of music, and wasting of water that accompanied my sweet Luke.
Come back and yell at me,
tease me,
berate me,
fill my senses with your sounds and smells.
I miss you.
I can't accept you are gone.
Infuse my life with you once more.

What will happen with my love for you,
all my endless love, where will it go?
I want to hold and touch you.
A luxury I can never again have.

EULOGY

I have now seen with my own eyes Luke's body. Cold and still, so tall, such strong limbs, such strong hands.
My magnificent, proud boy.

But it is only in the touching that I can truly verify that it is him, touching and sensing as I did the moment he was handed to me at birth, I repeat the pattern in his death.
It is indeed my Luke.

I hold and hold his hand, drinking the feeling in, so that I may remember it always, for soon I will not be able to, nor ever again. I try to tap this feeling into my memory, to store the feeling eternally; that I may be able to recall it, but I can not remember how.

I kiss his forehead, his cheek, as I did so often in sickness, in happiness, in gratitude and in pure love. But now it is in parting, an emotion for which I have no description.

I had not planned to speak at Luke's funeral, partially mute with distress as I am, but later as I lay in semi consciousness the tears that swell from beneath my closed lids form sentences as if the words were written on each tear.
The words of what Luke is to me, the words of my loss, the words of my anger, the words of my warning, words that had not yet appeared to my conscious mind but now, here debut upon my tears.
I record them as they form.

I read them over and over at each memorial, Boston, London, Los Angeles and each time they ring true
They will ring true forever.

Luke is MY son
He was my Empire State of Mind.

As a family we were drawn together, we were all
soul mates....And now our four is a three.

The outpouring of love from around the world has
and does mean so much to me.
But your collective love of Luke
does not hold a candle to mine.

On the Tribute page, I see how you all bathed in
Luke's sunshine, his kindness, his laughter, his loyalty,
his love of life - his smile.

But Luke was also a fragile boy
... and some of you knew that.

For 23 years I have **fiercely** protected his fragile soul.

Every boy who has taken risks with his life
Should be scared. And every mother is afraid.

The true tribute you can all make IS....
IF you are ever lucky enough
to meet another boy like Luke - STOP, THINK!

Maybe they are not as strong as they may seem
OR as strong as you
Maybe YOU are not as strong as you think *you* are

and maybe, just maybe ....

GEORGE'S BIRTHDAY

No sign of life in my psyche.
Too confused to drive or speak or cook.

It is George's 21st birthday.

A day to celebrate,
But his heart is broken. His brother gone. His family at sea.

I recall the last time we were so at sea. When Adam and I separated, our marriage in disarray.

George's response on that October day some ten years ago, when we told the boys their Dad was leaving, was visceral.

He promptly proceeded to draw up the guest list to his upcoming birthday party, as if when all his world was broken apart, the safe haven of familiar tradition was sought.
We three sat together around the kitchen table and the 40 invitations were crafted as if nothing had happened.

And so today (and last night) I was his Mum. His normal Mum.

I can not perform the most basic of routine tasks and yet:
I stayed up all night to bake the traditional cakes of George's birthday, fresh cream éclairs.

Fuck knows how.
But here they are, in all their glory,

The first sign that I am in here. Somewhere.

10

It has all been about Luke.
But I am George's Mum too.

Glorious choux pastries with shiny chocolate tops.
The symbol of this Mother's fight to tend to her child.
Where I thought all love was eclipsed.

The first normal thing I have done.
And I did it for my child.
Driven by love.
A Mother's love.

Will that same love, that drove me to this dark place
eventually be what sets me free?

I DON'T CARE

Dearest Darling Luke,

59 days ago you died. Can't think of any words, I love you, I love you, and I can never have you in my arms again. I'm heading east on a plane again, this time to England. It was to be a time for advent and fun, but there's no fun. Just sorrow. I yearn to join you. I cannot imagine a life without you.

Take the plane down.
Take me with you.
This is no life.
This is what happens when you let go.

I never got to say goodbye, but I would never have wanted to. I did want you always to be with me. I just want to hold you, to touch you, to hear your noise, your laugh, your chatter, your stories. For me, there is no feeling left in the world.

No excitement
No joy
No laughter
No love

Just a desperate blanket of nothing where I cannot find you.

Luke-O-Bean, come back to me.

Just about to land at Heathrow, watching the TV show *Friday Night Dinners*.
It reminds me more of what we lost; we lost our family.

12

So intertwined were we that with the one lost, we are all lost.

I have come to London to sort out my Swedish passport.
I don't care about it at all.
But once I did; so maybe one day, I will again.

But for now, I don't care.
About this, or anything.

EQUINE GRIEF THERAPY

So brittle, so fragile, disoriented.

My hearing so sensitive that the sounds of everyday life assault my senses.

Unable to hold a pencil in my shaking hand. I barely breathe, my heartbeat not perceivable. Silent, small and anxious, I am driven (as I can not), for Equine Grief Therapy.

Luke and I had a private world together in our horses.

A world of wonder, laughter, tension, hard labour and often conflict. He would shine in a dressage arena, a magician on horseback. Two champions blending as one. A connection so strong between boy and horse in their daily work, a sight to behold.

And now I travel to meet a herd of rescue horses, once saved and now saving others in despair.

A horse's survival depends on a higher level of intuition, a connection to the spirit world, whilst simultaneously at one with the earth. For an early warning is their only effective defense in nature, beasts with such a powerful forcefield so far reaching, that will naturally choose flight over fight.

The herd responds to my presence immediately. I have their attention, kicking at the fences and whickering at their first sighting. The preliminary safety talk does not interest me, as a death by their action would be merciful.

In the midst of these beloved creatures my body stirs. Memories and senses flicker.

I am introduced to the Mustang.

A creature of legend to Luke and me.

He courses his teeth across my crown, pulling my hair upward as I crouch at his feet, his power palpable.

My first ever Mustang and he is tending to me. Then all at once he returns to his hay. He is done.

Outside three chestnuts are divided in two paddocks. Calling me.

One stands alone, the others paddocked together.

They are separated by a small ditch with a wooden bridge.

I am torn between the two paddocks.

When I go to the solo horse the other two call me but when I go to them they walk away and proceed with normal life.

Returning to the solo horse; they call me back.

Back and forth over the divide, I am displaced.

Hovering over the ditch. I cannot choose.

I begin to see the pair as Adam and George, who call me away from the lure of joining Luke but only want me back to resume normality; and the solo horse is Luke, separated in death.

An allegory for a Sophie's Choice: to choose between my children, George (and Adam) in this world craving the return of their lost mother and wife, drawing me away from the world after life, where Luke is alone.

I choose the solo horse, for Luke did not like to be alone.

To be separated was always torture for him. Turning my back on him, he could not bear. When I would ask him to leave the house when he was using, he would not last long. He would return and stay clean a while, abstaining so that he may remain in the fold. A tactic I had abandoned for the pain that it caused us all.

The chestnut caresses me, blows and snorts and falls at my feet and rolls (an equine clearing mechanism), as if he is clearing my pain for me.

He rises and approaches to chew on my 'Luke' ring, a beautiful gift from another Mother in Luke's memory. He wants it gone. I remove it.

He proceeds to my sleeve, to uncover a bracelet given to me by my beloved Coven, a symbol of solidarity from my dear friends; an homage to Luke. I remove that too.

He is satisfied and proceeds to lead a game.

A game that I know, but one he has never been known to play before.

A game of blowing in each other's nostrils whilst gently biting my hands as I scratch his teeth. Blowing back and forth face to muzzle,

the game quickens. I reassure the uneasy therapist.

This is the game that Luke would play with all his horses, but especially his beloved chestnut Pluto. She is transfixed.

My joy rises.

I feel love.

I've not felt a sense of fun since the moment that I heard Luke was gone.

My reflexes sharp, as we deftly play on this knife edge.

I am lost in it, we are at one.

I was not dead, yet I could feel Luke in me.

I was here with my feet on this earth and I was with Luke too, his playful spirit, his sharp wit.

Is the gift from the equine world to me, to show me that not only can I feel love, life and the quickening of my pulse again but also the knowledge, now palpable, that, like an equid, I too could have

a connection to the spirit world, whilst here on earth?
I do not have to choose.
I can have both.
I can have Luke AND George.

The jewellery symbolising my first shock and grief, cast off so clearly by this connection, is a metaphor not lost on me. In this fleeting moment I feel it.

Uncertain of what is to come, I shed my first stage of grief.

REGRET, CONFUSION
NOTHING LEFT OF ME

Reading on the Tribute Page, I see how other people saw Luke.
Fun, smiley, full of hugs, laughter, adventure.
Now I finally can enjoy him fully.

Where others saw fun,
I saw danger.

If I heard laughter,
I would be afraid.

The fragile boy full of anger would come home to me.
We could not completely enjoy him.
We were always concerned.

We are left only with the contradiction of enjoying the images, words, videos posted by those party to his self-destruction. I could be angry at them, instead, we are grateful, so hungry are we for images, memories, voice recordings, anything! We voraciously watch over and over, we leave comments, we respond, we participate, released from the responsibility of considering the inevitable mess that we would have to clear up after witnessing such hijinks. No longer do we need to fear for him.

Where are my principles?
Nothing left of me. Total identity-loss.

Luke was:
Angry with me.
Hated me.

I was the one who would rein him in.
He wanted me off his case.
We had a dreadful fight a month before,
Such unkind words
Or was it a cry for help?

When you spend your life with children.
What is your life when they go?

My son is dead, he's bloody dead.
What is left of me? Half of my soul?
No job. Identity change – not a mother of two.
Luke had been my job, protecting his fragile soul.
I'm anxious, broken,
I cannot draw.
Who can I be?

Who is Sheila?

WAS IT A SHOCK?

Did I know all along? Mixed with guilt.

Too dark for me. A mother with hope no more. How can I get out of this?

I miss the adult man. I spent a lot of my time on him.
He texted me resumés, advice, both ways.
Stories, humour.
We would talk about Adam and George.

How can this be my life? How can this be my family?

My son is dead
My heart is broken
My spirit is broken
My family is broken

George lost his brother and the closest relationship he had.
He also lost his parents to grief.
Adam lost a son, a wife.

I lost all feeling apart from pain, panic, anger, despair, sorrow....
....and who wants any of those?

Adam used to say it was annoying that I was always so happy!

I know it won't be long before I lose all my friends and family who will tire of my grief and my husband moves to start another family elsewhere.

20

"Put it in a box to one side, so you can function," my sister once said.

I did think about why this sounds so absurd to me. It does also seem like a good idea, so why is it seemingly impossible?

Because.

Luke is part of me, was, is, always will be.
If I put "this" in a box to one side, part of me will be in that box too, leaving only part of me here. I am only a small part of who I was before.
Luke's death stole my life. What is left?

The love and grief is part of me now, as is Luke.
I will lose myself so easily now.
I can't put myself in a box to one side, there is so little left.

LEFT ON OUR OWN
BEING ALONE TOGETHER

The doors shut and the company of friends and family is over.

The thundering silence prevails, hearts become heavy and we are left with the weight of the truth of our new life.
The distractions gone, and Luke is still gone, still dead.
The former comfort of our private life as a family is gone too.
The curse of a lost child.
The five stages of grief spin like a roulette wheel, or the barrel of a gun – denial, anger, barter,
... each take their turn, or fall upon us all at once, all together.

Sometimes we are philosophical.
Sometimes we are proactive.
Sometimes just broken.
How will this ever seem better?
How will we ever cope?

Suicide is often the most comforting thought – practicality and logic cast aside.
We don't seem to be able to comfort each other.
All so sad, so deep in grief. Maybe a hand on a shoulder is all we have.
The comfort of my family gone, being alone together. Once so happy, now is so unhappy.
The loss of my family that I fought so hard for, protected so doggedly, is part of the tragedy we live. We used to love being together, now it just reminds us of what is gone.

The happiness we shared does not translate from four to three.

SHARED SOLITUDE

In bed. Shall I sink into unconsolable grief
or should I turn away from it.

The Facebook Tribute page calls. Films, pictures, soundbites of
Luke are our addiction.

Seeing what George liked, a posting from another room.
Is he crying too?
Should I go to him?
The Facebook page is almost the only way we three communicate
about our collective grief.

So shared, yet so solitary.

The familiar sniffing of Adam who lies next to me crying.
Nothing I can do to help.

SEX

Trusting in the world, in Luke;

I had to let go. I had surrendered.

The last night of Luke's life we were feeling light, happy, and very serene.

Our boys both away, both doing so well, we ate out and went to bed happy.

The house was upside down and we were sleeping in Luke's bedroom as we were decorating ours.

We awoke later and made love. I have no idea what time.

I told Adam that it felt like the night we made Luke.
He agreed.
Later that day, we both realised that we were making love as Luke was dying.
Autopsy may confirm otherwise, but for now,
how will I ever make love without that in my mind?

Feeling the person coming into life
as well as leaving, as they extinguish.
Is this what we were feeling?

Were we feeling Luke's soul?

WAS HE MINE TO KEEP?

Was it too much to ask him to be sober for my entertainment?

Today I am angry. Angry at him for taking the drugs, for not listening to me. But had he still been here, what form would he have taken? Angry, fiending, frustrated, high, stoned, coma. The grief is so immersing I think of little else.

Now I feel the wave come over my heart and I am sad and lost. I guess he had achieved everything. He knew he could make it as an Assistant Director and more.

-He knew he had the potential
-Maybe that was enough
-And being high was the priority over the future
-It was his future after all, although his death has taken my future too.

Had the thought of dying, of taking an overdose ever crossed his mind?

The risks, did they seem far off? Just as when I smoke a cigarette. His world was so light and happy, and yet I find the world of his drug use so dark, so far from the world I live in.
I live in that darkness now too. My mind running over the how, where, and why of it all.
The what-ifs...

My entire body lives in a state of cramp, anxiety, I don't breathe well. I can't think well.

My clothes no longer fit. I am heavy, I don't recognise myself inside or out. I am lost.

Was he mine to keep?

I know he was all grown up... but he wasn't.

He lived at home, used me as an excuse.
He always said he was never leaving home.
Was I a moderator that failed him?

In the happy videos on Facebook, I see he had a world that I could not, nor should not be part of.

So was the end of his life really to come when I let go?

WHEN I HEARD
THE WORDS

There are phone messages on my phone dated the 1st of October, 2016 at 11:59.
They are the first calls, the failed attempts at bringing us the news.

I can neither delete nor listen to them. I will one day, just not now.

The call came on Adam's phone.
It was George, agitated: "Mum! Is mum there? Why is she not answering her phone?"

"I'm sorry I was doing stuff, the ringer was off. What's going on?"

"It's Luke! He's gone!. He's dead!"

I hear those words, cast from my young son's mouth, not yet 21, telling us that Luke is dead.
Oh please world, turn back time! Please, no no no.

I cancel my hair appointment.

But those words ring through my head, my heart, my blood, my soul - over and over.
They will continue to do so
for months,
for years,

forever.

JUST FOR NOW

For now, I will agree to stay alive.

I cannot bear to leave my mother to feel as I do.
Too cruel now that I have the knowledge of such pain.

My husband, my other son, would be freer without me.
Without the constant reminder of what we have lost.

My sister will understand.

FAMILY UNPLANNED

I am back on the plane. Another plane in a series of planes.

I sit once more next to a stranger. Lovely, charming gentleman.

What was once charming is now a danger. Tales of his family and grandchildren at Christmas.

Oh please, don't ask me.

I bury myself in my journal and stare at the sun setting over the Alps.

How will the future look for me?

We only have one living son for Christmas in the mountains, so much focus on one son.

Not the rowdy mix of George and Luke interacting, laughing, helping each other – their lives at odds, or not. Their little cousins playing, caring for each other. NO. One living child from two living parents, George now carries the mantle of only child. Not only has he lost his brother, his mother, his father, the structure of the only family he has ever known – but he now carries the one hundred percent focus of his parents. No diversions from his brother.

I never wanted that dynamic. I always wanted Luke to have a sibling.

Two children together.

The perfect balance of our family is gone. My mother, who is an only child, always said that being an only child should be unlawful. She is in awe, bemused at the sibling relationship. The immense unconditional bond between Anna and me, how would it be to lose that?

To watch her daughters and my sons together. George will never have this again.

He has become an only child, and Adam and I the parents of one.

(One living, for I cannot leave it unwritten, nor unsaid, that I am still Luke's mother, and Luke will always be my son.)

So how do we stop that overly anxious setup that is a single child and parents?

That preciousness, that suffocating, imbalanced family that I never wanted for either myself or my family.

If I drop out of the world? ....What then?

A widower and his remaining son? ....How does that look?

Is it better than: The two hearty over-attentive irritating parents in red coats and fine sweaters, anxious, too much focus on their one precious son? No diversion. No balance. No other son visiting at Christmas. Nobody to share the burden of aging parents.

Dear God, how did this all get so fucked up?

I had it all, and now I am lost. I am done.

Why do I have to keep being?

Robbed of what I earned and fought to keep, over and over.

Am I, too, to be broken over and over?

And why do this to George and Adam, and for fuck's sake Luke?

Or is this some master plan?

Luke's and my mission to return until our work is done.

Oh Luke, what is that to be? Show me!

Chest full. Stomach full. Heart full
Torso of stone
Hanging on the edge
No comfort
Always at the tipping point
Too hard to bear

This is now my life.

TOX REPORT

Adam received the tox report and results of the heart autopsy.

Now I realise that I'd been hoping for some other cause of death.
Against all evidence, and heartfelt knowledge, I wanted it not to
say what it did say.

Acute opioid intoxication, including heroin.

Heroin killed my son.
Nothing else, just heroin.

Well there it is.
I thought I didn't carry the prejudice of others. The stigma.
But I realise now, that the word heroin carries an immense dark-
ness for me.
I am rather numb, rather still. I am silent.
I do not want to release this massive pressure in my chest.
I want to scream and smash things up.
I am angry at Luke.
But I remain still.

Wanting to wait till we speak further to the Medical Examiner, be-
fore I unleash it.
Before I fully allow it to wash over me.
Before I allow it.

At least they say it's a pleasant way to die.
A warm orgasm of death.

So am I released now from overwhelming grief?

At this very moment I feel that I am. Because I am furious.

It's starting to rain. I'm pissed off because I want to smoke another cigarette. Sitting on the table, feet on the chair, as I did so often with Luke, just chatting.

I want to know how often he'd tried it.
The dose, so small, it was likely to be the first outing.
But it was enough to kill him.
How did he take it? Did he smoke it? snort it?...... inject it?
Did he take it because he could not get the stuff he usually takes?
We know from his phone that it was 30s he was expecting.

I do feel a release from the inevitable life of living with a heroin-addicted son and all that entails.

I sit bemused at the stigma I feel.
Because in this moment I do feel it. Dark, heavy, dirty.
If I sit with it long enough, feel it, examine it, will it help me understand the stigma of heroin? The root of it?
Why does it feel so different from other drugs?
Oxy, Norco, Percs, heroin - it is all actaully the same.
All fucking opioids. So why does it feel so different?
If I can understand my own feelings of stigma, maybe, I can understand where it comes from and so help others to overcome theirs.

Would Luke have remained a high functioning addict for long?
Or would his dreams of success in the film industry have been taken over by heroin?
Anger is driving me forward to take care of my living son, who has led a life seemingly so different.
I'm going to fold George's laundry.

Lose this extra weight I have laid over my bones.

Get myself together and decide what to do with my information from this report, Luke's phone and what best to do with his memorial fund.

How can we help those who do not want to be helped?
Do I really still want to tattoo my body with Luke's name?
Christ, what a waste!
But Yes!
This is a disease, Sheila!
A shitty fucking disease.

I will celebrate that lovely man.
I will go forward with all that is good in my life.

For now, I want no signs from Luke.
I know he is sorry for the pain he has caused us all, but he has made his decision to do what he wanted. Help was here if he wanted it, and he chose heroin. His disease chose heroin. The love of being high overtook all his sensibility to live a life of work and career and family.

Yes, I want it to be someone's fault, and in a way, there's much at fault. I will find my part in it too. But for now...
He was doing what he wanted to do – experimenting with drugs was part of that.
I am sorry Luke if I was part of it.
But most of all, I am sorry that I have lost you.

Off to fold George's laundry and talk to my loving Adam who has been the hero in this awful tragedy.

For now, I am back.

"See... he smiles when you hug him."

AN IMPRINT,
WHERE LOVE ONCE WAS

(Thursdays are bad for me)
After spending three days with a dear friend and her children,
whom I helped birth, I realise that I actually feel nothing. I see the
children happy, they kiss and hug me,
I feel no joy. No love, No wonder.
I see my dear friend, so dear, she's like a sister - but nothing.
But what I do feel with Elin, as I do with my own sister, is safe.

The notion of another baby, is gone, not because of my age, but
because I feel no love.
The photograph of George smiling whilst I force an embrace upon
him, so artfully captured by Adam, a man who can express more
emotion in a photograph than in words or physicality. This photograph, now my screensaver, evokes a glimpse of emotion in my
heart, as I see George's smile, I see my love has meaning to him.
Adam saw this, captured it, and showed me "See... he smiles when
you hug him."

The first feeling of a reason to go on. The pilot light that may
reignite my heart, my love of life. A flutter at the sight of this. If
there is a flutter of love, an imprint, where love once was, maybe
it can be restored? Not the love of a man, or lover, but the love of
happiness, the glimmer of what I used to be, have. Not an intel-
lectual love, but an instinct, a fabric of my being, torn fabric. Without that love there is no beauty, no appreciation, no hope, no
future.
It's as if I am not here, just watching myself be here, a burden to
everyone.
One tiny butterfly in my heart.

35

SAY HIS NAME

Movies have lifted our family, always. It was one of the things we all enjoyed and brought us together. When the boys were small, Friday night was movie night.
When they were grown, it was Sunday night.
We'd catch a movie and eat dinner, in no particular order.
Later as ex-pats in LA it became our Christmas Day activity - the excitement of new releases on the last possible date for Oscar consideration. We all loved it.

Luke was entranced by the language, the music and the images even as a small child and was in a cinema in his first year of life. Not bound by the way one is supposed to behave, he stood at the front with his tiny box of raisins and was silent and transfixed. Only returning to our side for the scary bits.

Making films never broke that spell for him - he just soaked up the magic of how they were made possible, the teamwork, the camaraderie, the logistics, the technical wizardry were all just more magic to him. He loved his job.

And now, tonight, on movie night, as I lay staring at his Tribute page, which sadly had fallen silent, eight miles away at the Golden Globes; his name is called. As if somehow, in some way, his name was always destined to be called.
He is dead now and all his big plans died with him, but tonight Billy Bob Thornton says his name.
Billy receives the Golden Globe for his role in *Goliath* and accepts in Luke's memory. Not just Luke but "Luke Scott". But more than that - he stands and tells the room of movie glitterati and millions of television viewers that Luke knew what he was doing - that he

was great at his job, made him want to come to work, and he loved him.

A mother in grief just wants to immortalize her child. I certainly do. I cannot bear to think of the day when people stop saying his name. It's all over our grief groups - say their name, say their name.

There is now a finite set of scenarios with Luke's name attached to it and a finite amount of people who will know him. Billy, in his gracious and highly public honour, has just expanded that number. Millions hear my boy's name and that he was brilliant! Because he was.

The Facebook blows up, my phone too. The images and footage of Billy on stage and backstage saying his name and describing the experience of Luke are posted over and over.
The Twitter storm follows, journalists seeking, 'who is Luke Scott?' His name repeated over and over again. They can find no obituary, they cannot find him on the International Movie Data Base.

Luke and I had spoken about that. He hadn't put up a page - he was waiting till he'd done bigger things, not just a PA. He had planned so much more. And now our friends are here, rallying, calling in access codes and dates, job titles, creating his IMDb page - I sit outside smoking, cognac in hand, writing, and watch the frenzy, testament to how Luke managed to create such professional recognition, such adulation from the lowly post of PA, so magnificently executed.

I am distraught, churned up, disoriented, proud and so sad for the loss of my wonderful boy who had touched so many, had so much support, so much talent that he could not fail to succeed. The waste of it enrages me.

And so they find me. A mutual friend can no longer stand that the best PA that Hollywood has ever known is left a mystery and he lets on to the Press that he knows Luke, us.

Will I agree to be interviewed?

Urged by Luke's image, crystal clear in my mind slapping his palm with the back of his hand, smiling.

"Mum! C'mon! I'm busting my balls up here!- this is it! - Billy has given you the stage … it's yours. Go speak, go tell our story."

.....and so, to *The Hollywood Reporter*, I do.

THE LIES
OF THE PEOPLE AROUND HIM BECOME THE TRUTH. THE POLICE REPORT

The police report came. I read it last night. When your child dies of an overdose, he is treated like a junkie (which he was). His truth is not his own. The lies in the police report unsettling.

The lies of the people around him become the truth.

The police report is sloppy. The police report does not make sense. It's a mass of fabrication. Adam is misquoted. Witness names misspelled and their stories neither hold nor fit with what they actually told us. Their cowardly fabrication becomes the enduring final truth of my son. The truth of how he left this world. A sloppy, cowardly, self-serving deceitful truth. Nobody cares, just another junkie on a bedroom floor, why bother?

The reports that we see now, three and a half months later, over a quarter of a year later, could have been of some use to us at the time. Clues for us, the only ones who could benefit.

Why so delayed? The cold reality is oddly settling. The gaps that they cannot fill in are clear to me now, and so I will have to try to find them myself. Plans, imaginings of conversations fill my conscious and subconscious brain.

The irony of an alcohol swab to prevent bacteria whilst death was administered into his blood. Where was his brilliant mind in that moment?

Did you inject it, darling?

How do I get Marlon to tell me? Why is it so important to know?
Injection, snorting, smoking... he's dead. Why do I need to know?
It was Luke's choice, it was his prerogative.
It took his life, It was in error, but it was his to take,
as mine is mine to take.

Again I marvel that I miss and grieve for him so hard.
I miss the true Luke, not the one who was so angry, but in truth,
I miss him too.
Any version of Luke is better than no Luke.

So here I am, waiting at my first medium meeting, to take the only
version of Luke that I may have.

I love you Luke.
I wish it could be different,
but I'll meet you halfway, because that is all I have.

Can you meet me halfway, right at the borderline
Is where I'm gonna wait, for you
I'll be looking out, night n' day
Took my heart to the limit, and this is where I stay
I can't go any further than this
I want you so bad it's my only wish
                                          -Black Eyed Peas

IN MY STILLNESS

I am all right, at peace.
And at the same time, I am far from all right.

If I just stay in my breathing, and in my stillness, I am safe.
As soon as I have to engage outside that, I am full of anxiety, fear
and have no will to live.

I can barely take one step at a time ...
I actually don't think I can make the rest of my life - this marathon.

After therapy I understand that I have a dark side and a light side.
In the dark side lies the obsessing about the events that took Luke
from his life.

The light side is the sunshine,
the flare that is lukelove and all the joy of life that he brought me.
The light is where I'll live,
I am casting out the dark.
I can get it back when I need it.

GRIEVING AS A FAMILY

Well, now I see the complex issue of healing and grieving as a family. The reaching out to George on Facetime yesterday, the submission of hope that we may help each other, in his wise words, in defining that fixing up the bedroom that was once Luke's – the way I was going to do it, to surprise Luke upon his return – to still do it is "... not moving on, Mum; it's moving forward."

My resolve, my wish to keep the light in my heart – is challenged tonight by Adam's despair; that this grief will always be with us. His fear that our plan to help in this awful epidemic of drugs will keep us locked in the memory of how we lost our son Luke.

We are all eternally locked in the dread of this loss.
One of us may at any time find solace,
yet another may feel despair or anger,
another indifference,
each swirling around in our emotions, in our unfathomed grief
– so tangible and so abstract at once.

In my mind, the joy of Luke's smile. The memory of times of sobriety that gave me hope.
The dark days of treading on eggshells around him wondering if it would be over,
.........but not like this.

The pride of watching him work, and the appreciation of his colleagues.
The imagined images of his final moments.

A LETTER TO MARLON

Should I dare to write the letter to Marlon?
Not to send, but to see if my anger is relieved?
Well, here goes...

Marlon,
Although it is hard for me to blame you totally, where was your
conscience the night of September 30th or in the early hours of
October 1st?
I have read your cowardly, self-serving lies in the police report,
the scene cleared of all evidence, save a baggie, empty and dis-
carded and the sinister alcohol swab left on the table.

Did you care enough to protect from bacteria, yet not to stop at
injecting death into my son?
You didn't watch over him: who knows what careless regard you
had for his life, or indeed ours... which have been sunken into
depths of unfathomable despair.

You lied to me, you lied to his father, his brother and to his friends,
even though you knew that the truth would be found out.

You laid a line of lies that led in many directions,
but all away from you.

You have my pity that you have no honour, you drank my tea and
stared into the eyes of a grieving mother, and lied. You can never
undo what you have done.

Your disease keeps you in the grip of deceit and you have done
this many times.

My family, for which I fought so fiercely, is taken from me by your actions, love so strong, a bond that is shattered, lives fragmented and all in search of euphoria that only ever leads to hell. Hell for you. Hell for everyone that your actions have touched. I would wish you a painful and pathetic life, but you already have that.

I hate that you live whilst my Luke does not. I rue the day that you ever met.

Is this weird enough for you yet?

There is no worse life I could wish for you than the one you already live.

But a thing that you cannot understand is that in accepting Luke's death, I see a terrible disease. And as I accept this disease in Luke, I accept it in you and all the other enablers around him. Like any disease, it strives to live on and pass itself from victim to victim, each of you encouraging each other to succumb to its claws. The call for more slaves, insatiable, immortal, the disease lives on even after you die, the disease voraciously moves on to the next, no care for its host that has given so much for it. It has taken Luke's life as it did so many before him, using each of you as its instrument and casting you to one side, no reverence for life nor love.

Addiction is its name, and here you were, its deadly instrument. Pathetic and helpless to its power.
Until you stop it working your hand you will continue to slavishly do its bidding in death. Luke is free now of its dark grip. You are not.
I will not let it take me nor drag my family into its dark shadows, that threaten happiness and joy.

You have hurt my soul in your doing.
You were entrusted with my firstborn son, through a false friend-
ship, and you were careless with his life… and for what?

Your master rules you. But never me.

I will never grant it hate, but I do wish it had taken you the
months before Luke ever came. A fleeting chance that you may
not have lived to kill Luke.

I hope you and your addiction live happily ever after. Unlikely, but
that's your choice.
                              Luke's Mother

Letter done.

At the point that I came to write, I realise that my anger towards
Marlon is not real. My anger is with drugs. The grip that they have.
The addiction that they breed, like a virus, that merges with the
soul, casting regard for life aside – a demon possession.
Satan itself.
A power so strong that life has no meaning, not yours nor theirs.

Addiction has taken so much from my life and will continue to do
so, the focus of my past eight years.
Not only has it taken Luke, it has hurt my soul, my family.

I hate it! I hate it!
And somehow, it cannot be destroyed.

Eternally afflicted by addiction.

45

THE CALL I WISH I'D HAD

It's another Saturday. It's 11:57. This is when the calls were about
to come in and break our happiness. A happiness in ignorance.
Ignorance of the irreparable death of my son. Sweet Luke.
Ignorance of how my firstborn is already dead.
Ignorance of how opioids have taken his brain,
first in addiction and now in death.

Why did nobody warn me about the opioids, the OxyContin, the
Xanax, the Norco, the 30's?
His friends knew. Why did they not tell me?
...... and yet, now I have knowledge of how far his friend has
sunken into the claws of OxyContin, his brain almost certainly
rewired - he will not be able to quit without help.
And yet, I have not yet made that call.

I have tracked his mother's contact details.
Why is it so hard to call her and contact her with this news?

This is the call I claim so hard that I would have wanted in
advance of Luke's death.
Setting aside the questions of 'what could I have done?',
MAYBE I could have done nothing.
But also, who knows what turns an addict around?
Maybe another mother can?
Without the knowledge, she is in the dark.
As was I.

I am anxious about breaking her heart with the despair that this
knowledge surely will bring. But whilst her son is alive, she has
more chance of helping, than if he is dead.

What harm can I do?
Save the harm of hurting her?

I hear my own cry in the dark. 'Why did nobody call me?'
...and the tears fall.
And now I need to call her.

I am frozen.

Do I message her to call me?
Do I just call cold?
Injecting my terrible words into her life unannounced?
Is she driving?
Is she safe to hear this? Is she ever safe to hear this?

I am baffled at my weakness at this moment.
All at once I forgive those who could have called me -
this is not an easy action to take.
I have reached out to the boy. He won't call me back. I have said
that I will talk to his family. Ten days have passed and, in truth, I
am glad he has not called me. I can now call his mum. Did he want
me to call her? ...Maybe.

I left messages in several places.
She called me back.

She was grateful, or at least she said so.
I cried.
She asked what she could do for us.
I said that I did not know, but to tell her boy that I am not angry,
.......and that Luke loved him so.

She will keep me updated.

ANGER, GRIEF, DEATH

Tonight – Adam is angry.

A familiar feeling enfolds the house, heavy and sad, and his anger fills the very air that I breathe.

Can I tolerate this? And my grief as well?

His grief, of course, in the form of anger – an unbearable future lies in wait for me.

More and more, leaving this world appeals.

Death, please take me.

WHAT WOULD HELP?

I was visited today by another of Luke's friends.

Rather, I summoned him after reading on Luke's text chains how far in danger he too was with his using. I had considered calling his parents, but he took the option of talking to me.

These boys are over-therapized and know exactly what you want to hear.

But after I called bullshit, the conversation took an unusual turn.

We spoke of his struggles.

His anxiety comes at night when he's alone, away from his using friends.

All his friends use.

He told of how rehabs at their high cost (for life saving treatment) make him feel even more of a 'douche bag' for costing his parents so much money.

He loved Wilderness Camp, the most meaningful of all his treatments, and would love to return. A unanimous view held by Luke and all the friends who had completed Wilderness.

The therapeutic boarding school that Luke attended after Wilderness did indeed cost a fortune and the buildings were lacking - the dorms reeked, always too cold or too hot - impairing much-needed healing sleep.

The school was institutionalized, dingy and drab, grotty. The food was less than mediocre, all of which evoked a message that they were of no worth - and they heard it.

The climate was one of a remand school, they were each mistrusted and soon taught to mistrust. To mistrust the staff and each other.

A report from a student that may save the life of another or halt inappropriate staff behaviour was encouraged formally but, in truth, it was perilous, considered 'snitching', and retribution would, in some way, follow.

These were high-school children.

Not children who were trouble, but children who were troubled.

The very institution that was supposed to be helping them find a sober way of thinking was teaching them the opposite. It was cruel and harsh, not by design but by default.

The NA rooms followed with drab environments, terrible seating and flickering strip lights. Surely these people are in enough discomfort internally without external discomfort too.

With the heightened sensitivity of early recovery do their senses need a further onslaught?

Another message screaming that they are worthless?

I get it - the AA system is paid for in dues, not sponsored, and they should be looking within for their power, but it is flawed for young adults looking for a brighter future in sobriety.

I get it - the schools take a high physical toll but they cost a fucking fortune - someone could just whizz off to IKEA and make an effort for these young people so displaced, disoriented and far from home.

A nice place to be helps our thinking. Natural light, nature, warm and dry, bright and airy. The premise of any architectural theory.

And when they are wigging out in the dead of night?

When they are back home resisting their old friend group and its destructive patterns?

If AA doesn't work for you - if you have no sponsor?
Where can you go and be safe and have company?
Others to talk to?
We are not solitary creatures.

Many speak of the loneliness of early sobriety.
Having to find new friends at a time when they are most
vulnerable.

In my deep grief I, too, find the demons of the night intolerable.
It would be lovely to meet someone for crêpes and share our stories now at 3.30 am.

An App? Like Tinder - not for sex or love but for someone to go
to the movies with, or to skate-board with, get a coffee, someone
else who is trying not to get high.

Does sober fun have to mean yoga and kale smoothies?
Christ! - they got sober - not personality changes.

Sober bars and clubs have no way of making money without the
booze.
No dancing without booze? Hmm... interesting message.

Newly sober people rarely have any money.
Is it really all about money at a time when so many are dying?

Is it really beyond us to find a solution to this?

With the 23 million Americans in recovery, can't we pool our
brains, our energy, our resources? Stand proud of sobriety
achieved in darker times and come together to show their own
bright futures and how they cope in this absurdly fast-paced

world - sober? Show and tell.

Can we not cast off the shame evoking anonymity and put faces to this disease, show the human side, the hope? Stop the stigma.

We are not all rock stars or trailer trash - we are lawyers, doctors, stay at home Mums, engineers, designers, chefs, architects, bankers, dog trainers, politicians, tech geniuses....
.....we are you!

What about helping with gainful employment?
Can we not put our heads together,
maybe a dollar or two?
...that would be $46m!

Whether we like it or not, delayed gratification is a thing of the past. This is a time where instant gratification is part of the psyche of everyone and everything, every business around us.
Could a successful solution to this insidious disease not incorporate that?

Do the newly sober really have to live outside our society?

Can we stop saying why it can't .....and start thinking of how it can?

FIND A CURE

Alone in the house.
The long-awaited call with Bob Shapiro is over in a trice.
Bob spoke to me as a courtesy to a mutual friend.
Bob lost his son in 2005.
He has a foundation. A successful programme: *Brent's Club*.
She thought we should speak.

I was hoping for some direction.
What needs to be done? Is there a forgotten angle?
Something that your foundation does not cover?
A call to action. A purpose in my hopelessness.

He told me ...."Find a cure".

Sitting in heavy silence,

I can hear Luke laughing "Mate! you don't know my Mum!!"
Luke, confident in me as a force of nature.
I used to be so determined, so vectored.
"Mate! you don't know what you've started!"
I can picture Luke grinning, slapping his palm with the back of his
hand, as he did whenever he was excited. Always believing in me.

I sit in silence. Broken. Not wanting to disappoint Luke, again.

Bob seems to think that the rehabs work, though they didn't work
for either Luke or Brent, both confident after lengthy sobriety that
a bit of booze would not hurt, leading them both, at speed, back
toward drugs and then; death.
Tales of corruption in rehabs, the paltry insurance coverage, doc-

tors who screw up the timing of Suboxone injections, methadone programs that dilute the dose for wider profit margins, the dismal treatment in offensive surroundings of sober livings, the vast costs. There's got to be another way. New ways for new times.

Feeling small. Feeling hopeless.

My phone pings.
A friend has sent me an article about Ibogaine.
A plant. An addiction interrupter discovered in error by a heroin addict in search of a trip, only to discover that it took away his quest for heroin for days without withdrawal symptoms.

Researching the web into the night. The blockings from the FDA, the success stories. A way to calmly visit the traumas that may have led to drug use or those during active drug use.
A system without the long isolation from society, in misery, in delayed gratification.
A reset button for the rewiring in the brain.
This is a shot at sobriety that Luke would have gone for.
Something I could have asked of him.
Dr Mash is leading the development, looking for a way to reach the people who need it.
"Legalised marajuana didn't come through the FDA, it came from the people."

I email her.
We speak. She has a plan, a vision, and it is great.
There is another way, an alternative route for those whom the current practices have failed.

I'm in!

JUST A
TERRIBLE ACCIDENT

Late afternoon; a bad time of day for me. Right now, on this day, I have an elephant on my chest. Or is it in my chest? Caught under my rib cage, pressing my lungs and my heart.

Yesterday my panic attack started as I left Erewhon, the only place I can bear to buy groceries, probably because it's fancy, small, light, but not bright, and seems to have daylight in it... or does it? Not sure now.

The house and garden feel dilapidated by the rain and the lack of interest I have in it.

I have not felt Luke around me so strongly and this makes me sad. Sadness blocks the connection I have read, and so I vowed to cast it aside in favor of receiving messages.

My health is deteriorating.

I am struggling to go to bed at a timely hour, so I am sleep deprived – and then everything goes downhill.

This morning I heard Luke call "Mum!" Or was it, "Hey Mum!"? An electronic-like sound as if on the speaker on my phone, and I loved it!

George is home, injured and involved with his new love. That's lovely to watch, but I can see he is not dealing with the death of his brother.

He doesn't want to talk about it or light his candle at night.

The dark thoughts that I could lose him, too, are overwhelming. Many have lost both children to addiction, either in them blocking their grief or in a normalization of drug use with "That won't happen to me." Everyone seems to think they have it under control.

Or will I drive George away because around me, he cannot forget, as I drip in the inability to function with Luke dead?

My anger develops towards those who did not support me in trying to keep Luke from advancing his drug use.
No support for his return to sobriety.
People who helped him cheat drug testing by recommending tonics, and those who knew he had moved on from just using weed.
What were they thinking? ...That I was just going to spoil his fun?
That I would throw him out of the house and not try to help?
What did they think I was doing?
Long after they have moved on, my life will still be shattered.
Luke means more to me than he ever would or could to them.
Did they even think?

As George became part of the 'Drugs are Fun Gang', I lost a great ally. Often it was he that would hint when Luke was struggling.
It was indeed George's impact letter to Luke in Wilderness that impacted Luke the most. The irony that this was imparted that drunken night on Luke's 21st birthday, all sobriety lost, dumbfounds me!

Losing George's disapproval of Luke's drug use seems key – although it would seem that Luke 'went dark' on George, too, after he told Luke that he didn't approve of the Xanax.
For fucks' sake, where was my tip-off then?

And Luke's BFF too? After the presentation of all the pills! He, too, showed disapproval, gave Luke a lecture, but did he not see that was the time for a call, to me? – so now, what of the other boy? –

He's had no assistance since the opioid usage.
Do I call his Dad?

If I don't call; does it make me as complicit in his usage as those around Luke were in Luke's?

Is this really the moment to mind my own business?

With the pathetic results and outcomes of rehabs, what hope is there? But discovery often seems to be the thing that turns many around.

"*A standing bare, at rock bottom, in front of loved ones.*" – said Davina McCall. Realizing that everyone knew.

Where was Luke's chance?
Did I miss it? Did we all just miss it?

High-functioning addicts going undiscovered through their addiction, people standing clueless to one side. The information was all there, but I had no clue. I had no knowledge of opioids, and the effect that they have - the irritation over the tiniest things – such a clue, I later discover.

How do we get that information out there?

Had I still been in therapy, I would have discussed the big fight that Luke and I had.
...... Maybe I'd have had a light shone on the clues before me.

But in truth, I had let go.
Let go of the chasing, in the hope that Luke would see for himself.
......Well that went well!

So, this brings me to the words of my friend Joy.
Words of truth and said with love, they are my mantra when the
sliding doors of fate come to crush me with the 'what ifs'.
She took me by the arms and stared into my eyes..

"Sheila, loads of our friends take loads of dreadful drugs... and they
don't die. ....This is just a terrible accident."

This is the truth I must hold onto.
The awful truth. Luke's life reduced to chance. But it is true.
He could have just as easily lived and found sobriety.
This is just a terrible accident.

Many take drugs, many take heroin and don't die.
Many do take heroin and do die,
and Luke was one of them.

It was just a terrible accident; the whole truth of which I will never
actually know.

So, all I have left, and it is not a little thing, is that I appear to be
lucky enough to have some intuitive ability and that will keep me
in contact with Luke in his spirit form.
The same spirit that has always been in him, from conception,
and that is a lot.

I will treasure that and enjoy him in the way I always did.

The nasty drugs gone from his body, and the pure sweet, funny,
fragile son lives on.
In me and around me.

CAN'T KEEP IT TOGETHER

There's no solace.
No place of calm.
I am drowning.
I can't find a place to go that feels bearable.
I can't feel Luke.
I know I can't still have a relationship like before.
But I wish I could feel him, hear him, see him.
Playful signs.
Please Luke.

Luke talk to me.
Luke send me signs.
Luke I love you.
Luke I miss you.

Are you breaking your balls out there to do this and I just can't
see, feel or hear?

Waiting in the car, sobbing outside therapy
Today I want to hear the unplayed phone messages from Marlon,
from that fateful day.
I can not bear to hear what he may have said,
I can not bear to delete them.
They eat at me.
My therapist and I will listen together.

TRYING TO FIND LOST JOY
IN THE SONGS OF LUKE

Driving, listening to *Empire State of Mind*,
trying to feel the joy that this once brought me.
The joy of Luke.
Of course, this will take time.

I cry,
I wail,
I sob.
I can barely sing along.

But some place deep,
I feel the lukelove.

> *When you are sorrowful*
> *look again in your heart,*
> *and you shall see that in truth*
> *you are weeping*
> *for that which has been your delight.*
>
> Kahlil Gibran

THE PASSING
OF AFTERNOON TO NIGHT

Each afternoon, having done my rounds of exercise, therapy, and
a visit to a tolerant friend who can stand the half-presence of my
being over tea and cigarettes, I find myself back at the same place
of loneliness in my grief. Alone.

I am, at best, exhausted and out of distractions and brought back
to my loneliness, sitting and waiting for the tears to engulf me.

To bring the tears on would seem an easy thing.
A fine gossamer, brittle barrier lies between my expression and
tears. A wisp of memory may catch me and the barrier shatters
to reveal this all-encapsulating sadness, and sometimes it comes
with a smile. A smile at the thought of what I once had, the tears
for what I have lost.

And what have I lost?
I have a home, a loving husband, a loving son.
Both broken and lost in our new world that we are at every second trying to emotionally and physically navigate, build and recre-
ate. Once we were four, now we are three. It's unfathomable and
a treacherous road to walk.

This family lost at a whim, in a trice, in a second on one decision.
I no longer know how to walk into a room.

Before, I was a woman with two sons, but who am I now?
A woman with one son? An only child?
Or still a woman with two sons?
How many children do I have?

It is not about how to define myself to others – the truth is when people ask how many children I have, the answer is not so much complicated to answer but complicated to know.

The crying continues, but to truly cry into the deep sadness requires, for me, today, a weepy film - An emotional sticking of fingers in your throat to release this torturous grief. I search for *Truly Madly Deeply* and I cannot find it. So *Collateral Beauty* it is.

I sit in solitude on my sofa. Sitting and hugging myself, watching. My soul rushes up through my body, giving into deep howling and engulfs me in the loss of my child and life as I knew it, surrendering me to a power so deep.
Oh! Luke-O-Bean, my Luke!

This display of my grief is exacerbated by my solitude, but in truth, can only really be accessed in privacy. Such surrender is hard to accomplish if witnessed. Too painful to show to myself, let alone another. What do I want? I don't even know. I want the impossible.

I want Luke to be alive.
I want Luke to text me or call me.
I want to hear his voice, his chatter.
His tales from a day on set, a night out,
or his opinions about anything.

I want to not have this veil of sadness that filters anything and everything I see, hear, do or experience.
I know this will never be over.
This grief will cloud everything forever.

I don't love George or Adam any less because Luke is gone, but the joy that they bring is tainted and sullied by the loss of the bright and fragile life that I brought into this world, the joy and pain of being Luke's mother, in life.

There is nothing in my life that wasn't touched or shared by Luke. Music from happier days makes me remember him (and even music from my youth reminds me of my optimism for a life ahead, and that saddens me for what my life became).

Restaurants where we ate and chattered.

Streets we drove on, streets he navigated me to take, for Luke was better than any traffic App.

The roar of a fancy car that he admired.

The sight of a dreadful car that he would diss.

Beaches, and even the sky. His photos on his phone, full of stunning sunrises that he would capture en route to early-morning set calls.

The stars at night – the eternal celestial reminder of more optimistic times. The night we spent under respective tarps in the Utah desert at his graduation from Wilderness. A sober, clearheaded boy and I laid and looked up at the sky as he pointed out each constellation, highlighting each of the extra stars that are not visible at home in light-polluted skies, (in later years he would point out Orion's sword, also visible in Mammoth, navigating it with the description "It looks like it's his dick, Mum." – that would always help me find it). He told me of the long nights in Wilderness, looking up at the heavens, seeing the taillights of planes, wondering, imagining who onboard was going on holiday, and hoping that it may be the plane bringing us to take him home.

Oh Luke!

So where can I look?

Where can I cast my gaze to not have reminders of what I have lost? The answer is simple, ...there is no such place.

For me, Luke is everywhere because he is part of me.

One day, in fact even now, I am glad of this.

But one day, I hope that these things will be there to remind me of what I had.

For now, that same experience reminds me of what I have lost.

What we have lost.

What the world has lost.

I cannot ever remember a time that I felt so disconnected to the universe.

NIGHT – SAME DAY

Sitting on my deck, arse on table and feet on the chair, cognac and cigarettes, pen and paper. I imagine the feeling I had when he was imminent – a text to say he was on his way, the roar of his engine approaching, the blip as his car locked and the clatter of his arrival. His giant form appearing around the corner of the house. The sound of his voice as he greeted me. The thoughts and suspicions I had about his whereabouts all turned out to be true. That he went other places before he came home from work. Once leaving home at 9:30 PM on a Sunday to drive two hours to buy drugs saddens me so.

How could I not have found a way to reach him?
The ramblings of every mother who lost a child to addiction.
A series of hits and misses, sliding doors,
the dwelling on the "if onlys" of life.

My heart seems dimmed and faded and it is a known fact that a grief-filled heart beats weakly.

Each night I visualize my SA node, nature's pacemaker, dimmed and indifferent. I allow its vitality to dim further and hope that by morning it may have given up its impertinence to keep signaling. I hope to never wake and let myself be taken to be reunited with

Luke. To be allowed to exit a life that feels indeed like a prison sentence. What possible good can there be in my living on? I consume air, water, food, money, all the things that could be better allocated to those who want to stay here on Earth.

I can see no possible good in my being alive. I am broken, I am irreparable. What use is a sad lump to the world? I bring no joy to others. I contribute nothing. I am a waste of Earth's resources. I have organs that could be of use to others, maybe to save a young person or a child, but Lord knows that my lungs will be useless.

So here's a question:
If there is no reunion with Luke for me in death, would I still go?
Or is the thought of ending this pain enough to be tempted?
Well I'm still here, still breathing, still my SA node fires.
So what is keeping me here?

I must find a way to do good in all this.
I will never engage in my life in the way I did before.
That life is over.
But I will find a new purpose.

Luke, show me, show me my new place.
Give me a purpose, other than draining the world of cognac and English Marlboro Lights.

My vulnerability and sadness have given me a voice.
Let's not waste it, show me.

LUKELOVE TATTOO

I am still outside, drinking cognac and smoking in solitude
and I realise it is Pancake Day (Shrove Tuesday)
a day that used to be one of excitement. No longer.

My fringe in my eyes, stinks of cigarettes. My veins laced with expensive cognac.

So this week is the week of my tattoo. What does this tattoo symbolize?
My tattoo will put an indelible mark on my pulse closest to my heart – a mark that reads:

lukelove

An expression, a phenomenon, coined by Luke.
When my phone would freeze or the stove would not light; he'd help me. When I would ask what he'd done he'd reply
"It just needed a bit of lukelove"
For all things work better with a bit of lukelove.

So does lukelove have any caps? Is it two words, or is it one word?
It's a phenomenon.
It will make anything work,
anything happen,
anything better.

It's there to show the world that I am marked by this phenomenon. It's a signal to the world that I am different, I am changed, I am touched by lukelove.
Lukelove, once you have known it; is indelible from your soul and

your heart.

This tattoo will be visible to me to show that I am touched by it and, above all, as Adam pointed out, people will ask about it – an open invitation to talk about Luke, and that can only be a good thing.

George suggested that I add a rose – a rose to symbolize the rose sleeve tattoo that Luke and I had mischieviously planned for me, in life. An entire sleeve of roses, decorative and, all at once, slightly sinister.

It will also always symbolize the rose that I placed in Luke's hands at his cremation.

Although I have lost Luke, I will always have known, and will continue to call upon, the phenomenon of lukelove.

I love you Luke, now in death, as I did in life.
My love is eternal.

The day I die, people will see at my cremation, and in handling my corpse, that I was lucky enough to have known, be touched by and felt lukelove.

Luke, I hope you felt my mumlove, ...then and now.

THE MEMORY OF TOUCH

My panic is that I cannot remember what Luke feels like.
I held his hand at the funeral home.
I held it to feel if it was him, to know it was him on a cellular level.
Aware that this was my last chance to drink in his form.
To feel him.

I tried to tap in that feeling so I could have that last forever.
And now, I can't remember, and I'll never feel him again in his
physical form.

I realise now that we remember how it feels to touch our children
because we touch them every day.

At first, when they are small, we touch them all the time.
All day every day.

As they grow, we touch them at intervals of the day.
Help them dress,
maybe just tie their school tie,
pick nits from their hair (not Luke, he never had nits. His hair was
so thick that we would joke that they would perish before they
could find the way into his scalp.)
we bathe them,
help them with a wound,
or just nuzzle into each other for a story,
sit close as we do homework, just touching arms as we sit adja-
cent,
tie on boots,
ski bindings,
sit in a pile watching TV.

The intervals of physical touch change as they grow.
As adult children, you touch less.
Greet with a hug,
lark about, playfighting.

Recently, Luke would ask me to tie up his unruly hair for work,
so we would touch then.
Or help with a stubborn spot (zits); we'd touch.
Sit on his lap at the garden table for shortage of chairs.
We would touch.

And so, those memories of touch stay with you, ever reminding
and banking the sense, the knowledge of the touch of your child.

The memory has an expiration date, it would seem.

I haven't held Luke's hand, touched his form, since October,
maybe the 8th. And here I am in March, the memory of his touch
fading, slipping away, like a dream upon waking – it's sort of there,
but I cannot put my finger on it.

I cannot actually recall the knowledge, and I'm left in panic and
despair.

SATURDAY AGAIN

Yes, it's Saturday again. It's 12:10. The memory of that first Saturday re- runs...

Luke was dead and people were spreading the news, trying to find our contact details to tell us what we should never have to know.

Today I woke anxious, that somehow I drove Luke to drugs, and his eventual death. I can't work out, as my instincts are gone, how to be a mother to George or a wife to Adam. Afraid that I will drive George the same way, I wonder if it would be better that I die. From my grave I can do no harm.

I spent yesterday gainfully.

I volunteered to help with Sandy's school function, which is tonight. I was in myself, my able, professional self. I have to admit less impaired, but rather more honest about my abilities, clear about what I do know.

My friends are sweet, supportive, and somehow "get it" on some level. Accepting that I am never more than a breath away from despair. They seem unafraid to love their children with all their soul, and so brave to be so close to me at this time, which must bring such horror to their hearts.

The evening was spent with one of Luke's friends, a hairdresser from *Goliath*, part of a team that brought him much joy. She lost her own mother two months before she lost Luke, and before that, she lost her brother. She knows grief.

We sat talking with her dog at our sides, of death, autopsy, police reports, sorting possessions, of grief, joy, smells, spiritual experiences, horror, ashes, making ashes into gems versus diamonds, memories, what-ifs, if-onlys.

We talked for hours, exchanging experiences, asking questions of interest and of emotional inquiry.

It dawned on me that in finding each other at a time of matched grief, united in our circumstances and by Luke, that we are lucky to know each other at this crossroads in our lives, different and, at once, the same.

At many points I have asked the cosmos, "Where was Luke's Sheila?"
Where was the person who would say, "Hey Luke, this drug thing is no good. It has to stop."?
The person who may call his attention to what he was doing and maybe help him stop.

I see that she may be that person.
It just hadn't happened,
it just wasn't time.
She never knew,
he hid it from her, as he did from us all,
but I am clear that when the time came, she would have been one of them,
if not **the** one.
I think she may have been his Sheila.
It just all happened too soon.

Tattoo rescheduled (after cancellation by artist) for tomorrow,
Thank you Cosmos.
Thank you Luke.

NOT ENOUGH

It breaks my heart to think that Luke may not have felt my unconditional love in life.
In truth, I am, in life, incomplete without him.

He is my firstborn, and I felt complete the moment I knew I was pregnant.

I have grasped and fought for his fragile soul.
We have formed unconventional pacts and deals to help him.
Everything was, in the end, not enough,
or not effective enough to heal him
or to drive addiction from his soul.
Abaddon, angel of destruction, you got him in the end.
I wasn't enough,
and now, I am lost without him.

FADING MEMORIES

Heavy-hearted and full of tears that never seem to stop flowing, I have a wave of grief that flows across my being.

Identifying why I'm so especially sad today is not easy.
It has for the past few days been intolerable.

A fading memory of his touch, his voice, his true likeness in actual motion, what it feels like to hold his hand, to receive a hug, his smile, his laugh, his anger, shouting, his advice – what it is to hear his mind, his stories.

A photograph, a video, it would appear, serves as a reminder, a suggestion, but without the top up of Luke's actual presence, the photos and videos lose their power, they have no offering to re-mind me of Luke in life.
As if the two-dimensional image only has true likeness, when one's memories fill in the blanks.
The image is not accurate, it just reminds the memory of what it is to see Luke, hear Luke, watch Luke.
When the memories fade, as they seem to be, my brain cannot make sense of those images. It cannot complete them, for it has lost that which would complete them and so the images are less and less representative of Luke.

My darling boy, Luke-O-Bean, each time I lose something I feel new grief.
His body,
his soul,
memories of his touch,
memories of his sound,

memories of smell,
memories of movement,
I grieve each one,
each sense lost,
one by one.

So as my memory of Luke and me get farther and farther away
from each other.
I will now stop moving forward,
stop moving away from Luke,
'til I can figure out and secure a way of taking him forward with
me.

I cannot bear a life without him, so I will find a way.
Memory is not solid enough,
not stable enough,
not enduring,
but I will find a new way.

In truth it would appear that I am approaching the mourning period that is called isolation.
I want to be alone with my thoughts, with Luke, and here I am
about to embark on a journey to London, to sit next to a stranger
on a plane, then living in another person's house.

I just want to be in the *stoge* garden; me, Luke, and cigarettes.

A PARALLEL OF TRUTHS

Some time has passed since I've written.

I've seemed to have taken a little holiday from my journal, and maybe from my grief, although it is true that it is always with me.

I've been to London to celebrate Anna and Simon's 50th birthdays. Adam wasn't sure if he could come, not sure if he could dance, celebrate. But I wanted to celebrate the people who rushed to our side when we needed them most.
And I did.
As did he.
I danced, as did he, as did George,
I cried and danced, safe in the fold of our family, generations deep and their friends, who were all aware of our tragic loss.

The message they all seemed to want was:
"What can we do to prevent our children falling to the same end?"
I have been baffled by this, that I am some type of expert – ME?
Wait! – the woman with the dead kid.?
Maybe advice should be sought elsewhere.

But now I see that they are maybe asking me for the insights, the 20:20 vision of hindsight. Without realizing it, I had a thought. I imparted the thing that I do know – beware of marijuana.
In the cloud of marijuana, I missed the signs of opioid behavior; the short temper, the restless irritation, indigestion.
I put it all down to the exhaustion of work, the weed and the frustration of being a young adult at home.
For this, I may never forgive myself.
For now, this is the only 20-20 vision I can offer.

I am also learning that indeed we are capable of many opposing feelings at once.
I am feeling angry,
sad,
loving,
distraught,
and relieved all at the same time.

I am settling into this and allowing myself to feel this all in parallel,
no longer an expression of conflicting thoughts, but a parallel of truths,
safe in the knowledge that they are ALL the truth.

They have a forward vector now, smoothly running on rails.
For they are all true,
and cannot be denied.

So, I will sit with them, and take them forward in my quest for peace.

THE FB LANGUAGE
OF GRIEF

In the GRASP (Grief Recovery After Substance Passing) Facebook group, we share our awful stories, our daily struggle and words of hope.

Rightly or wrongly;
As I read I evaluate them and think to myself
"This one's worse than mine,"
or
"This one's not as bad as mine,"
or
"Thank God I dodged this."

We offer each other comfort, words of wisdom and validate each other's thoughts and emotions.
Sometimes we just use an emoji.

Within the limited language of Facebook, our reactions are limited to symbols, to which we reassign meaning, in a new language of Facebook.
The "like" symbol, the heart symbol, the broken heart symbol, the series of emojis.
Of course we don't *like* their story or *love* their story,
but we transpose without prior arrangement that we send love, or that we hear them.

We hear and we are heard
And it is comforting.

DIFFERENCE BETWEEN
ADDICTION & DEPENDENCE

I read there is a difference, but I still have no way of knowing which of these Luke had.

There's a searching inside of me that wants to know what Luke's daily life was like.
Did he take Oxy, Norco, Xanax, Adderall every day?
Did he need it to start his day?
Did he need it to end his day?
Did he need it when his back or knees hurt?
Did he use it to keep withdrawal away?
Did he use it for fun?
Was he still enjoying it?
Or had that passed into the dread of needing it?
Even if he did not want to.

Did he know?

REMINDED OF
LUKE'S BEAUTIFUL SOUL

So much further down the line – thinking solely of what life must have been like for Luke in his final months, weeks, days, hours, minutes, and seconds. Obsessed by this darkness. And then...

I am reminded of the true beauty in the soul of Luke, in the form of a letter that had strayed in time, only to reach me when I needed it most.
A printed letter inside a condolence card from the mother of one of Luke's dearest friends. A letter reaching from soul to soul, one mother to another.

She met Luke once and he made her feel special. That was Luke. She spoke of Luke's heart, full of love, and congratulated us on raising such a being,
but in truth, that was not us - that was all Luke.

In the letter she addresses what I cannot bear to be true, that there is nothing that can reunite Luke and myself.

She reminded me of what I have lost, in her compliments and observations from her fleeting encounter.

Dear Adam and Sheila,
I only met Luke once, but that does not describe the impact he had on me, specifically because of the way he influenced my relationship with Ryan and Ryan himself. Ryan and I were separated after a custody fight –like the story in the Bible with the two mothers fighting over a baby that Solomon threatens to cut in

half. I let go, but there was no wise Solomon to give me my child and Ryan and I were separated. I had a nervous breakdown that lasted what felt like a decade, believing I had lost my son forever. When I finally made my way back to Ryan he was fifteen, failing high school, desperately needing me and also hating me. As connected as we are by love and blood we have had a hard road to mend our relationship as mother and son. Ryan has been taught to view me as crazy and there is a lot to undoing this. A particular issue was him learning to drive my manual Mercedes which seemed to be important to me only. It is a safe car, a beautiful car, and a rare car, but Ryan viewed it as worthless junk and thought there was no reason for him to learn to drive it. Then one day his attitude started to change.

He asked me to teach him to drive it. He was afraid of the hills by my apartment at first, but then he got more adventurous. He started to see the many benefits, how much fun it was, how connected he felt to the road, the way it forced his brain to be concentrating on driving all the time. He stopped listening to the radio, only wanting to hear the sound of the motor. Parental engineering was finally working.

When I met Luke I realised the influence had come from him. The conversation Luke and I had was all about cars. He agreed with me and validated me and thought my car was a great car. Ryan just smiled and nodded.

I reached out to shake Luke's hand as we were saying goodbye and he kissed me awkwardly hitting my ear. He was so much different than any friend of Ryan's that I have ever met, so evolved, so loving, so engaging. He made me feel special. I am in awe of the both of you for the love that was in this boy. It was inspirational. You are inspirational.

When I was separated from Ryan I hung on to the fact that even though we were not together there was hope that someday we would be, and that he might still love me. I also hung on to the *fact that even though I couldn't touch him or kiss him, at least he was safe and alive. But for that, I had no will to live. I've cried many tears for the two of you this week, I'm crying now as I write this, because I know how hard it is when that is all you have to hold on to; I can't imagine how hard it is when that last hope is gone.*

I wish that I could take a portion of this pain from you, in gratitude for the beautiful child I got to share for a moment. I can't. I'm so sorry. But I pray for you, that you hold onto each other and to George the way Ryan and I have been holding onto each other this last week- another gift from his amazing friend Luke.

I will never again hold Luke's hand, I will never again feel his hugs, I will never again hear his philosophical point of view, I will never again hear his stories.

How tragic it is to lose a child to addiction, for this extraordinary son was obscured by drugs for some time, on and off, in the months before his death.

What a pity, a travesty of our love for each other.
And so, all at once, I feel the loss of my boy.
But so proud, so happy, that the legacy of lukelove lives on in so many hearts, even in mine, broken though it is, and so I enter a new thread in my grief journey –
hoping he is safe and happy, and at peace where he is now.

FIRST AND LAST

I found Luke's 20-week scan today;
the first time I ever saw him.

The last time I saw him was as they closed the door on the cremation furnace.

The first sighting and the last sighting sit side by side in my heart, sandwiching the memories of his wonderful soul.

My wonderful boy.

ULTRALIGHT BEAM

It's Thursday and my spirit is sad.

Listening to Luke's music – the stuff he played for me.
Trying to remember the joy that I felt.
Him leaping around with me, without me.

Early one morning as Kanye's *Life of Pablo* album dropped -
"Mum, you're gonna' love this track." –
the house shaking as Ultralight Beam soared into the air
across my senses, raising my pulse and the hairs on my nape.

Oh Luke, how I loved it!

Oh Luke! ....and now
you brought me to playing Kanye on my own in my car!!!!!! ... Mate!

Driving
Sobbing

Trying to call him to my side, *Ultralight Beam* thrusting into the
LA air from my car.
Roof down. I reach to the sky with both arms... screaming
"Come back Luke!"

ARE YOU THERE?

Learning to live without Luke, in human form, will be my life's work. Learning to stay in contact with him from beyond will be my greatest project.

The work I feel we have to do will be the masterpiece of my loss – the completion with him at my side in spirit form.

I spent the day yesterday in his bed, and, as I have for the past two days, played *Life of Pablo* very loud in my car, in my head, in the house, calling him to me. Remembering his excitement.

Ultralight Beam soars. And yes! I loved it then! I love it now!

I use it to try and sense him, to try and feel what it was to be in his presence.

I have lost my connection with his spirit, or at least I have lost the strength of connection that I had before. My therapist tells me that this is a transfer from the physical presence to the non-physical. I have lost my confidence that what I sense is indeed him.

"Mum, I'm right here. Right here," is what my senses hear as I write, and as I doubt.

So, tomorrow I am off to see Austyn Wells, my medium, to see if I am getting it right.

A skilled interpreter to affirm what I am feeling, to confirm that it is true, or not.

I am looking forward to spending the afternoon with Luke and hearing any news he may have. Hearing his wit, his turn of phrase, his way of seeing.

Hey Luke,

Will you come? Luke will you be there? I hope so. But not if it costs you.

    Mum x

AN AFTERNOON
WITH LUKE

I spent an afternoon with Luke last week with Austyn.
The best description I can offer is that I speak a bit of French, but
Austyn is fluent.

The events that lead to Luke's death were discussed, and the people were identified, not by name, but by description.

My path forward, our "projects", were discussed. What I should
do, what I should not, and what is too dangerous to touch.

It leads me to question: do spirits misdirect in order to save face?
But I am happy to take his direction: after all, I did ask!

His beloved brother and friends are mentioned by name. One
who I was going to contact, but must not, was too.

An accurate image of the girl he loves forever was given, and as
requested, I will tell her. The circumstances of their breakup
given. I knew that was part of his decline, but I wasn't clear if it
was because of the breakup, or the cause of the breakup, and indeed it was the latter.
"It should have been his wakeup call," he said.
The drug use ruined that, the thing that he treasured most.
He says he was an asshole.
Oh, poor Luke. He had it all, but could not keep it.

In some ways, many ways, he had more sense in a single hair on
his head than I have in my entire body.
He is the voice in my head. I sit writing in his spot, identified by

Austyn by the markings in the newly laid concrete.

So what of me?

The realisation that I will never call his name and that the 'for Luke' to-do lists are now finite, steeps slowly into my veins, and slowly, drop by drop, I truly realise that he is gone.
But never forgotten.

I feel him at my side and indeed I call him, say his name, as I would before, Luke-O-Bean,
the precious gift of lukelove,
both given and received,
will live on, as long as there is a breath in my body.

And whilst we are on that note ...

SUICIDE

As my dear friend battles with criticism of her groundbreaking show, that, to me, identifies all that is dysfunctional in a young person's world – rape, abuse, drugs, shame, suicide; I see
Nic Sheff, my absent mentor, the original *Beautiful Boy*, defended her cause and wrote episode eight of her show, *13 Reasons Why*.

All at once, my worlds collided. Nic's book *We All Fall Down* was my bible, my hope, during Luke's life – relapse is part of recovery – lines that I revisited for hope and clues and guidance, and now, my battle to save my son and my desire to end my own life collided in Nic.

I finally wrote the letter that I so often and so long had wanted to write. That Nic had seen me through some dark days and nights, and now, through depicting the heroine's suicide, stopped me in my own plans to end my endless suffering. Or maybe postponed it.

How bad would it appear for Joy's own friend to end her life, whilst she is defending her choice to show a suicide does not cause a contagion of copycat acts. It is true. The graphic depiction gave me no sense of peace or gothic beauty and so repelled me.

Joe Biden explains the thoughts as,
"We have been on top of the mountain and the realisation that we will never be again is what drives us to suicide."

I will never be truly happy again.
My fight to always be happy (formerly achievable in the face of most anything, in my case) is lost.

I will always see the world through a filter of Luke's death.
To lose Luke to addiction forever makes me not want to live.

All the love and support, all the acts of true kindness help the days be bearable, but they don't change the intolerable pain of the interminable grief that I feel.

It's not personal.
It's not a reflection of anything external.
It's just a pain that is with me always, a pain so heavy.
A pain that only dying can cease.

For now, I will not do it.
Not for myself, but for George, Adam, and my beloved family and friends.

There's work to be done. I will go do it.
And then review.

JOINING DOTS OF JOY

It's six hours later, It's 2.00am and now I am in despair,
as if with my exit, my release now cancelled, I have no hope.

Do these heavy spells of despair come because I am not sleeping?
Or do the spells of not sleeping come because I'm slipping into despair?

Oh, Luke! Come back! Oh, Luke where are you?!

I am tired, but I don't go to bed.
I dread lying in the dark with my thoughts and this physical yearning for Luke. To see him, to hear him, to feel him, to put my arms around him, to stand on tip-toes and receive his hugs. None of this will ever happen again.

The trees bend in tonight's wind, and yet, I seem to be unable to bend, or lean into this dreadful truth.

As I sit here I can hear a car approaching in the distance.
My heart lifts for a moment as my physical memory thinks, in a trice, that it is Luke.
And in that instant - my grief lifts and I am light, I am happy.
A nanosecond of happiness.

What if I could capture that brief spark of joy, like a firefly, and hold it in my heart?

Maybe that's how I will survive - by not just thinking but feeling that, just for now, Luke will be back in a bit. Just as I would when he was away, at work, out for the night, in the other room.

I hold that tiny spark, that dot of joy, tight in my psyche.
This will take practice.

Will I ever be truly happy again?
Without Luke alive, my family incomplete, it seems unlikely.
But for now,
I'll join the dots of the fleeting notions that he'll be home soon.

WEIGHTED FOG

Did Luke ever exist? So far from him that I wonder if he was ever real. This is no life.

"Suicide should never be an option" – easy for others to say.
I am so desolate now that I have rejected suicide as an option, left stuck in my altered state.

Adam has asked me for more help.
I see him drowning in the finite to-do list of Luke's death - tax, cars, banks.
This seems reasonable, and I wish I had more to give. But it fills me with panic as I have no reserve energy. The boundless energy that I once had, before Luke died, the things that once seemed so easy, are now hard or impossible.
I am dragging an extraordinary weight with me always. A giant block of concrete that follows me everywhere. To lift a glass to my lips, to close the door, is an effort that I have never before encountered. To make a decision, to make a choice, is to swim through a weighted fog that leaves me with partial sight and impaired thinking.

Is this just grief?
or did I draw energy from Luke? – he certainly stimulated me.

I just want to do right by Luke, to find out what happened, to serve his memory, to keep him living forever in my heart and memory and continue to help others.
Luke, is this task too much for me? Or am I just impatient?
For this quest, I have boundless energy.

MOTHER'S DAY

Not normally a particularly special day for us.
But I guess it would be a day that we would come together.
But we cannot.

People sent messages, flowers, and let me know that they were thinking of me.

George spent the day with us.
We noodled about and whilst in the cinema, I did briefly feel connected to Adam.

My connection with Luke is clearly part of my lifeforce and now it is altered, my connection to life is obscured.

What a heavy weight for George to bear.
This is not fair on him, but his sweetness is a comfort.

The Compassionate Friends Bereavement Group has taught me that the siblings suffer watching their mothers crushed under the weight of the loss of a child, as they, too, mourn the loss of their sibling, their mothers and fathers, and the loss of the family as they knew it.

Tragic on so many levels.

THE REAL
WORDS OF DEATH

Today I have a weight on my chest so heavy that I can barely concentrate, settle or even breathe.

I wrote a text that I need something for Luke's probate.
The words - LUKE'S PROBATE.
In black and white on my phone.
A reality hard to bear.

Adam has dealt with all that.
Writing emails, texts with the words of Luke's death.
How does he do that?
I guess he has no choice, as I am unable.

HARSH TRUTH

I have weathered a rollercoaster of emotions.
I have discussed much of Luke's troubles,
and I find peace sometimes,
but other times I just wish it was not so.

I am often so exhausted that I can't even go to bed;
the effort that it takes to move at all, seems too much.

I meet people who knew of Luke and heard so many good things
about him – a guy that touched so many – it's hard to comprehend
that he could not be alive anymore.

I read another Facebook post about how a father looks realisti-
cally at the future of his son and how it would only ever have been
a rollercoaster of heartbreak, had he survived.
This is a hard but, likely, true scenario for us too.
It feels disloyal, to Luke.

.....and if he had descended from his high-functioning drug use into
the nightmare of non-functioning,
would all these people still love him?
Still miss him?
Still mourn him?

Or would it just be me?

THERE WAS
NO TIME FOR ME

Today I read a piece that mentioned Mephedrone, the drug that
Luke started on when he was 16 or 15.

It was a trigger. It's where it all began.
The reading out loud of that word to Adam choked me with tears.
Maybe this indicates that far beyond dealing with my present, in
the melee of dealing with Luke's drug use, I never took time to
deal with how I suffered, let alone where it led or where I am now.

Past trauma, even from this life,
the struggle to try and prevent his death,
continuous and never ceasing.
Always work to be done on me,
my reactions,
my actions,
and how best to help him

......all feels futile now,

the battle lost – did I help?
Did I make it worse?
Shoulda woulda coulda,
over and over and over.
The never-ending video in my head, heart and soul.
Too exhausted and burned out to help George.

LUKE'S BIRTHDAY

Luke's birthday has come and gone.
Luke loved his birthday.
I had to mark it, as ever, with a party with no one excluded.

Forty people gathered here to release the 200 butterflies that I raised from larvae and to feast on Eton Mess, a dessert that I make each year for Luke, just the way he likes it.

Last year it was so different.
"Hey Mum, I told the guys at work you'd make Eton Mess on my birthday."
"Sure, darling. How many people?"
"Um.....120?!!!" Playful sheepish eyes and a big grin.
He knew I would.

So, I separated 50 eggs, whipped quarts of cream, hulled 20 punnets of strawberries and Adam, George and I rolled onto set on the closed streets of downtown LA, where the security barriers parted for Luke's Mum bearing Eton Mess.

Everyone on that set knew Luke.
From the lowliest to the most powerful.
They all knew about us.
They all loved Luke
and were clear to seek us out and let us all know.

I watched as he worked through the night - he was here, then he was there - he tended to us - coffee - herb tea - food - answering the crew's questions as he walked and talked on his radio, answering one whilst instructing another.

Each person satisfied with his clear retort.
All executed with a huge smile and often humor.
It was a sight to behold.
And oh! How I loved to behold it! And yes, boast about it.
He was amazing.

This year's birthday was very different.
It was a lovely celebration of Luke.
But it is also a reminder that he will never come back, although
we will keep his memory alive forever.

Falling into despair and exhaustion, yet his friends surround me,
wanting me to help the cause, urging me to work on the foundation.

Why do they gather around me?
Is it guilt?
Why do they think of me as a badass?
I couldn't save Luke, but maybe I can save them?
Maybe it's not the mother's job to save their child,
maybe it's for the mother of another brother.
A friend, just one person who believes in them?
A new way forward?
Luke's love, his ex-girlfriend is so heartbroken, and I see how she
tried in her own way to save Luke.
It was not her responsibility,
she did what was best for her, and indeed for him.
Right there was his wake up call.
That's what he told me through the medium.
Gold stars to her.

Can I make my voice count?
How can I help them? In a way that suits them?

FUCK YOU!

It's Father's Day.
Happy Father's Day, Dad. Happy Father's Day, Adam.

The past week I have been so angry.
Rage is building up in my entire being.
Angry at the lack of support, for my struggle, the seven years before Luke's death.

To those who thought I was overreacting
To those who thought I liked the drama
To those who thought I was doing it because it was fashionable
To those who thought I was spoiling Luke's fun
To those who knew about the opioids
and thought they knew better
To the phrase "You've gotta' do what you've gotta' do"
To those who take weed lightly
To those who did not agree that Luke was an addict and defended him over helping him
To those who never read up
To those who did not help me
To the friends who knew he had relapsed and did not tell me
To the greedy pharmaceutical giants
To the lazy doctors who don't check what they are spoon-fed

I say, FUCK YOU!
Look at your part in this.
Look at my beloved, magical boy – DEAD!!

To the hopeless battle against addiction - FUCK YOU!
To shit therapists - FUCK YOU !

SERENITY REIGNS

After a period of lockdown,
unable to dress,
to eat,
to move,

Adam, in desperation
books me in for a treatment with Vicky Vlachonis.

A breakthrough of the blockage caused by anger gives way.

I text Marlon, and set up a meeting.
This is what has to happen.

Serenity reigns.

IT'S BEEN NINE MONTHS

Luke has been dead nine months.
The obvious thought is that it's the same amount of time that I carried him in my body.
He is still in my body.
Every tissue listens out for him, every sense is on alert to feel him.

The overwhelming need for the afterlife to exist reigns hard.
I hear him in my head, not an actual voice, but thoughts enter my head that are not my own.

But I have lost any sense of who I am.
I don't recognise myself internally.
The comfort that I once had, walking, talking, doing everyday things,
recognizing what I would want to do,
what I like,
what my opinions would be,
are all gone.

It's akin to the feeling that one is sickening for something,
as though flu is about to descend.
I am not totally present.
I am not totally enjoying myself, as if every experience is at arm-slength, just out of my reach. I am never really truly anywhere.

My brain soaked in a natural Xanax,
I don't remember names,
forget to check my email,
can't remember to do the slightest task, that would have been actually performed in my stride, let alone taken in my stride.

Next week I will fly to Boston to meet with Marlon.

Taking the advice of my therapist, who I sense is adapting to my journey; at my pace, sometimes slow, sometimes fast, but seldom hasty (a new turn indeed) and often very jumbled, I will focus on that meeting and that meeting alone, for it will surely unlock another wave of emotion, resolve, a tsunami.

George is home and working on *Goliath 2*. Luke's set.

The flutter in my heart when I hear he is on his way home has returned.

Absent till recently.

The joy that a mother feels when they gaze upon, or interact with, their child, that was once blocked by my grief, is now, once more, tangible.

The meetings with Luke's friends, searching for a direction for the foundation, remind me of the joy of Luke, bringing their energy to my home, helps call in the essence of Luke.

There seems to be a book in me, a book in us all. A joint effort of all our inputs, after all, we all had input in Luke's life. The exact angle is yet unclear, the exact tone to hit also foggy.

But for now, I'll prep for the impending meeting with Marlon, to meet in honesty and forgiveness is my approach. Let's see what that brings.

In the meantime, as if to give clarity to our mutual thoughts of 'shoulda woulda coulda', we have Marshall, Luke's friend, all at sea, his addiction raging in full flow. And yet, we find ourselves not knowing what to do.

We know he is in danger.

I have called his mother, and yet...

"Okay, let's play shoulda woulda coulda..." -
we couldn't help Luke,
and in hindsight we wish this, we wish that,
and yet here's Marshall,
alive still,
and yet what can we do?
Likewise with Marlon.

My premonition that Marlon will die before I get to him, taking with him the secrets of that night, looming as a danger, hoping that texting him may relieve some steam, and yet....
Oh fuck!....here I am again,
thinking I have some power over their addiction.
Will I ever learn?
Maybe.
But I will never stop trying!

NOTHING LEARNED

It's a hard realisation.

In meetings I have with Luke's friends - they are stoned.

They still use.

They think it's different,

They don't see the connection,

They think they are individual.

They think they've got this.

SUNDAY

It's so awkward in my home when there's just the three of us.
Luke's absence booming silently in our midst.
I don't know what to say to George,
and he has nothing to say to me.
It's awful.

MEETING WITH MARLON

Sitting on a bed, in a glorious house by the sea in Massachusetts, waiting to meet with Marlon.

What am I about to hear?
What am I about to discover?
What am I looking for?

Some peace.
Some closure.
The truth.

Nothing will bring my boy back to life. I would kill Marlon and eat his liver if I thought it would bring my Luke back, but it won't. I can hear Luke's voice in my head saying,
"Mate! trust me, you wouldn't want to eat *his* liver."

So moving forward, the fight for awareness against this disease, still so little headway made, still so many clinging to the concept of moral failure over a brain disorder.

So many lives ruined, both in life and death, to this disease.

The roadkill that surrounds it is far-reaching. The hearts broken, spirits lost, lives shattered.

What is the relationship with the substance that holds them so tight and comforts where the people who love them can't reach, compare to or win over?

Can I really help?

Am I so arrogant that I think I can find a new way forward where others have failed?

Or am I yet another victim who thinks I may divert the course and tame the beast of addiction? To this I say, with reservation, "Well I can try." But a new course must be set, one of love, lukelove.

I channel my Mum. I channel Luke. I channel my own power.

I call in my psychic ability, my motherly love. I beseech myself to stay calm, not be nervous, be myself, listen and think before I speak. My end-game, goal, may end up being different from what I may have originally thought, but I will give myself over to this meeting and follow the thread wherever it may lead, through a labyrinth, through the bowels of a tumbling wave, allow myself to be tossed about, taken into its power and spat out anew, having surrendered to its power. I can do good. I can make a difference, and I will!

Seven hours of coaxing Marlon to come and meet me, and now he isn't coming.

Will I hate him? He asks, why does he care?
I am launched into despair, crying, screaming, sobbing.
"Come back to me!" to Luke,
"Why?" to God.
I try to do good, and I really get no place.
I am bruised and battered by my turbulent wave that tosses me around, scraping my heart on the ocean floor. Cut, bruised, bleeding, concussed. I know not which way I face, which way is air. I surrender to its power, but the price is so high. How long will I be held under? Maybe it will kill me? Maybe I will resurface for a gasp of air with a renewed sense of life? Rejuvenated?

A DUTY TO
FOIL MADNESS

On my plane, homeward bound, on the tarmac at Logan.

The threat of becoming the Shakespearean mad woman is now real.
I woke last night in terror and despair. A high tensile wire snapped and unleashed, lashing out like an angry snake, spitting sparks and metal shards in my brain, in my soul – cutting my fibers. I was spinning, holding my head, chest pounding, no way in or out. All I could think was my mind has broken.
I just have to get back to California. I have to get back to Adam. I cannot be locked up in a madhouse here in the state where my son died.

Trapped back in a steel tube. Once more squishing my grief, my loss of Luke, loss of my family, and now I realise, loss of myself, into my economy plane seat.

Who knows what the new me will be? One thing's for sure, I don't know.

As I fly over the USA, memories of my life with Luke flood my body.
The Utah desert, flying on trips to and from the Massachusetts therapeutic boarding school, the whys; why did Luke not survive addiction? Was it addiction or experimentation?

Was it trauma that led him to use, to forget?
Was it usage-induced addiction? ......I missed so much.

Oh, that magical night in the Utah wilderness! He was so clear-headed, so funny, so bright.

I long for him, I yearn for him, I would so happily die to be re-united with him.

The pull to him is so strong, and yet, my life is not my own, for I share it, in an unwritten contract, with Adam, George, Mum, Anna, Rosie, Tilly, my friends, their babies.

And see – when I say I have nothing to live for - I do.

Not in the terms of something to look forward to,
but in the literal terms of "something" to live for:
The binding contract of obligation in marriage,
motherhood,
friendship,
family
and love,
..........to live.

PUSHING THROUGH

My brain falls silent.
The spinning in my brain remains.
It's distressing to me that it may represent lost connection, as suggested.
But I accept the suggestion for consideration.
How can I lose connection with my boy? No!

This leads me to think I must work harder on my connection, but I really am not sure how. I hear him tell me to journal, so I sit here in obedience, writing.
Evoking the episode that I had in the Boston night, the episode I call 'Shakespearean Mad Woman', brings me to nausea and motion sickness. Is this the place from where I should start writing, and let it flow? In an attempt to draw the episode, the discomfort and disorientation returns fast, and I find that I cannot really illustrate it, by any means.
Exhaustion floods over me, and I query whether it is just too much work to go there, and it overwhelms me with laziness and malaise.

Am I just not ready or in the same excuse of being *unable* to help an addict, letting myself off the hook just because it's hard?

People think I am brave and energetic, but I am often lazy and unable to push through, or, imagine a creative way to get past my blocks. Easily distracted by what seems easier, or more pleasant; evasion.

Help me, Luke, to reach a place and lose my fear that, my words will just be the banal ramblings of a grieving mother.

NOT READY FOR
OPEN WATER

My social incompetence is now becoming evident. A phenomenon I have seen in friends in early stage, as well as later stage, recovery.

Having socialized so much since Luke died, but with friends who
are so close to us, who may not necessarily know how we feel but
more importantly - maybe, that they are on the same timeline as
us.

Exposed at a party with people not-so-close, who had not seen
us since Luke died; it became apparent that their 'kind eyes' and
kind words left me looking for rescue. "Someone get me out of
this conversation." I expect it dawned on nobody, or maybe there
were no external signs of panic to see.

I felt like a social misfit – not interested in people's holidays, incapable of small talk, incapable of speaking about Luke's death and
the destruction of my family, as I once knew it and in clear view,
the loss of myself as I had known me.
I may look the same, or speak the same, but for sure, I am not the
same. I solved it by drinking heavily and hiding in the garden with
my cigarettes – although the out-of-step acquaintances followed
me.

Adam bailed me. We had each experienced the same discomfort
and so we realised that our friends and family have created a safe-
bay in which we may bask, laugh and chat (or not).
But we are far from ready for open water.
Good to know.

VILE CONUNDRUMS

For the first time today, when hearing another mother's troubles with her son, a friend of Luke's, I feel a relief that I no longer live the life of the addict's mother.

At the same time, I miss Luke's energy, smile, and companionship – but in active drug use, this is something that I always missed.

Missing the 'real Luke' is a pain that I have suffered intermittently for the past 8 years.

Now my task is the integration of these emotions.
- Missing 'real Luke', missing Luke in-body,
- Missing the hope for Luke out of addiction.
- Not missing the chaos that his addiction brought
- but the calm that it's over, is something to appreciate as well as to grieve.
- And as I have no choice, as Luke is indeed dead, embracing that calm, whilst continuing to recognise the magical boy that Luke truly was, and is in spirit.

These are the vile conundrums of a mother who loses a child to drugs.

NO SUNSHINE,
WITHOUT THE SON

The endless nights, like secret time, smoking and playing endless games on my iPad, mindlessly numbing myself into exhaustion, as if that's the only refuge from my thoughts.
Lost in time under the cover of night. No longer drinking alcohol, as that serves me badly now.

Waiting for a miracle – a sighting of Luke's spirit, and yet I am so disconnected from him.
Disconnected from Adam and George, lost in a fog, a silent fog in my wave, deep rolling wave. Will a sense of action suddenly come over me and show me the way forward?

Content in my solitude, as if company is a new pain, in which I have to behave in a way I do not want. Checking-out and content in my own madness. My Shakespearean sense of madness in grief – something has snapped in my mind – and yet, I don't care.

Break me, cut me, take away my ability to relate to others for I don't want to, nor need to anymore. My foundations for life are shattered in the loss of Luke. A loss that I do not feel whilst in this state, as if finally it has become too hard to bear.
The endless interminable fact that Luke is dead.

I gaze at pictures of him, his energy and overwhelming life force tangible, even in a photograph, as if to stare at them brings him to life.

Where can I go? Where can I go to find him?

Exhausted in my body and mind, the endeavor to seek and find him seems too much, even though it is all I want. Maybe because I worry, or think, that whatever or wherever I go – I will never find him. Is it only in death I will see him again? Feel his strong embrace.

Is it him I seek or myself?

I don't know nor feel myself for I know not what or who I am now, nor what I am to be.

Is sleep the boundary? Is sleep ever to be mine?

I love you Luke.

I loved you always.

I will love you forever.

Why oh why did you die?

And now the tears come rushing up through my body. When your heart is broken, is there no way to love anything or anyone else? Does your heart actually break? And with it does the capacity to love break too? I was once so full of love. I sat at the Hollywood Bowl tonight and felt nothing... nothing but the passing of time. The music did not move me, my warm and oh-so-supportive friends at my side, the warm wind of L.A. across my face as I drove through the stunning vistas of Mulholland Drive, and yet nothing. I observe, but I cannot feel.

There is no sunshine without the sun, nor without my eldest son. Is this my fate? A numb and detached state created to prevent the drowning in my tears. A million tears twinkling, beautiful tears all for my Luke. I wish I could meet with him in dreams or visions, or just anywhere.

I miss you Luke.

I hate drugs.

They take away so much from us all.

And now it's 3:20 am and George is home.
I will stop writing now and enjoy him.
I guess love is alive in me, yet I cannot bear that I will smother
George in the extra love that was once for Luke
... or is it just desperation?

TRYING TO BE
PART OF THE WORLD

I leave for vacation tomorrow with Adam, but not George.
I'm like an angry sick animal.
Angry and displaced.

It's too much to come into the practical side of life,
Packing, Passports, Taxis, Timings.
Part in the world, and yet still out of the world.

Constellation therapy came to my attention yesterday – a system
to realign yourself within your family. Where do we all fit, now
that a piece of us has gone?

Tumbling in my wave, allowing myself to take the journey whilst
coming away from my comfort zone. It's too hard.
Fighting with Adam, feeling like I want to get drunk.
Not a good idea when we are about to travel.

I will go back to my floating, and take the journey as it comes.

There was nothing wrong with Luke
If anything, maybe, he was,
for this world,
Too right

DID HE KNOW
HOW MUCH I LOVE HIM?

Sitting in the paradise of the rainforest in Costa Rica, it feels as though time has stood still. My grief is locked. It's hard to imagine that Luke is dead, or even if he ever was alive. How can it be that one loses a notion of him existing? Ever? And simultaneously no notion that he has ever died? In recent years, being away on holiday always meant, to me, that I would see Luke when I returned home. He would pick us up at the airport, have dinner upon our return. And what of George? I'm spending so much energy on grieving for Luke, whilst not knowing how to reach for George.

Many moments, every day, my mind strays to what would happen if I lost George too. How can I make an effective plea to the powers that be, to keep him alive? It's partially that I worry that it's because of me Luke died.

The reality of the most dreaded loss, that of losing a child, is now real to me. It's something that is no longer an irrational fear. It's the reality of my life now, the chances, the odds, the fragile line between life and death of a child. Yes, Luke's death, his chances of dying, were exacerbated by his drug use, and in the final hours, by using heroin, but how many people use heroin for years and never die? How many thousands, hundreds of thousands? Why could Luke not have survived that foray into heroin? Why did it have to kill him?

It's hard to be angry at Luke himself. I have no knowledge of what he was going through. Yes, I could jump to conclusions. Yes, I could decide it was his disorder running out of control, taking his brain to act in a way that would lead to his increased using. Or did he

117

just like to be high and want to experience everything? It's clear from his phone texts that it was not heroin he was expecting that night, or at least he was expecting 30's. Did Marlon bring contaminated or laced 30's, or did he bring heroin instead? Or did he bring nothing and later they went to get heroin as he was hurting/dopesick and so needed something and heroin was all he could get?

The dark secrets of his final hours will never be mine to know. The person with the answers will never tell, or at least is not ready to tell me yet. It's haunting. It never leaves me. How dreadful is the world in which I live? Thousands of other mothers feeling the same all over the world. Marlon's mother too - for the part her son played in the death of my son.

How will I ever feel at peace with these thoughts?

Such unfamiliar thoughts, emotions, restlessness at the core of my being.

If I could ever have one last meeting with Luke – what would I want to say or do?

Would there ever be enough time to say, do, or discuss what I want to?

Would I choose to use the time to unfold the mystery of his final hours?

Or would I use it to let him know how deeply I love him?

Would I want to know the truth that's truly burning me –

did he know how much I love him?

How proud I am of him?

How lost I am without his advice, opinions, humour and wisdom?

Or would I use it to find out if he's happy where he is now?

The secrets of the afterlife seem of little interest to me save, to know if he is enjoying it.

The tears flow now, and so, I know
the priority is not to know what happened,
but to speak of love and happiness and seek the knowledge that
he is happy.
The knowledge I can never truly have until I am with him too.

Is this why I think so often about and long for my own death?

UNABLE TO
FEEL THE GOOD

Why can I not be happy with what I have?
I have so much.
A fantastic husband and a wonderful son in George.
Both their lives shattered forever by the loss of their son and brother.
And the distancing of their wife and mother.

What a lot of "roadkill." For what, simply put, appears to be a dose of heroin.
Although drug use is so much more complex.

In my grief, am I now closer than ever, to how Luke may have felt?
Unable to feel the good things in my life rather than the bad?
Allowing the bad things to overwhelm the multitude of good?

What would it take for those things to turn around, to switch about?
For now, all I can do is hang here in purgatory.
Waiting for a direction, an emotion to take me.
Distract myself whilst I wait in the hope that I do no more damage to myself or to those who love me.

CALLING YOUR NAME

And now in Santa Teresa on the beach.

Feeling sad in a world without Luke.

Freefalling in sorrow and loss.

Nothing to grasp onto in a life of grief that isolates me in a bubble that only allows limited sentences through. Limited sound, taste, light, love.

The beguiling rainforests of Pacuare seemed a more sheltered, nurturing environment to me. The absence of western intervention, a stellar place. Preset meal times, activities within a safe and limited circumference. Fewer choices.

I can see how going to live in isolation would be a successful choice in grief.

Here there is music that triggers the sadness, the songs that remind me, not of Luke, but of the loss of Luke. Deep grief. I want to call his name 'til he comes back home...

Luke – what a lovely name

Luke – what a lovely boy

Luke – what a lovely man

Luke – what a gift you were

Luke – I am so sad you died

Luke – I am so sorry for everything I have done, or not done

The waves of sadness wash over me.

Distraction only serves to hold back the deep sorrow intermittently.

The energy to hold it back is as exhausting as the grief itself.

Taylor Swift and Zayn sing on;
I don't want to live forever 'cause I know I'll be livin' in vain,
and I don't wanna fit wherever,
I just wanna keep callin' your name
Until you come back home.

You think that you would understand what it means when someone dies.
But I realise now, that I do not.

I'm forever looking for signs, messages from Luke.
I'm still optimistic that somehow maybe
.....he'll come back home.

HIDING

In my grief
Intimacy is hard. Intimacy is unbearable.
Fearing those who can see into my dark soul.

I realise that at all of Luke's memorials, birthdays, and other gatherings – I hide in a crowd amongst people who know me less. Hiding my pain, my unbearable darkness, the fact that I am hanging on by a gossamer thread.

I realise that I had no idea about Luke's private life - his drug life. As his mother, I knew him better than anyone on one level, but not on this one.

Are these two things the same?
Me hiding the true depth of my despair and
Luke hiding his addiction and pain that lead him there?

The more we are hiding, the more we pull away?
In an effort to protect the tenuous systems we have in place to survive, do we pull away from those who love us most, those we love the most?

Do we pull away, distance ourselves, so that our darkness cannot be detected and in so doing, do we pull away from those who can help us?

Is this where Luke was hiding?
Where I now hide myself?

A BLOW TO THE HEAD

I'm waiting at my therapist's..
I've forgotten my credit card,
I've forgotten my diary (calendar).
I'm in her waiting room and there is no sign of her.
Door shut – so she may have another client.
So now I doubt myself but I cannot check my diary.
I thought today at 2pm or 3pm?
But I also took Tuesday at 4.
Was I clear? Was I mistaken?

I live in a fog where a successful interaction with the outside world is seemingly more by chance than by design. I wonder how I manage to drive. I wonder what makes some things succeed and other things not. There's no embarrassment in this, which is odd. I'm doing the best I can.

I can barely remember what it was to be the person that I was, always on the move and getting so much done. Now I scarcely do two things in one day, and if I do, it will surely result in forgotten credit cards, times, date changes, or driving in the opposite direction, missing turns, a lost sock. I'm in a daze.

I have taken a blow to the heart and it has the effect of a blow to the head.

George sent me a photo of my diary page, I am due here at 4, so right day, wrong time.

Should I remain here writing, or go?

Maybe Gracie, the cat, will come and sit with me.

The places that my brain has to go, I really was not equipped for this.

DEAD BUT LIVING

Sheila, the root of my being, is encased in a soundproofed world within me.
Buffering any true and real contact with the outside world.

My interactions with others feel like they are performed by a muscle memory from before Luke died.

Life is now performance rather than the world in which I live. This stops me feeling love and true connection like I am a boat bobbing along, directionless in an ocean, caught in my wave, deep in its roll, sound, light, touch and love are all on the other side of where I now live.

This shroud prevents me from heartfelt engagement. Inside my bubble there is just me, and sometimes Luke. Isolated, insulated, separated, like the massive headcold that I actually have, I can equalize my ears, but it doesn't actually change. The inner self, cut off. I am exhausted, I know I will lose everything that I once loved, but I feel like they are lost to me even if they are right here. Forced separation, a divide that I cannot cross. I'm blind, deaf, and dumb all at once. If I cross the bridge to others, the bubble comes with me and the arrival offers no change. I live a life with gestures and interactions learned by rote, but never felt. It has been this way since Luke died. Will it ever lift? And how will I go about making that happen?

Any thoughts by others that I am the same just prove my actions, words, and behavior are all well performed, but that is not me, just a mirage that I clearly perform well from instinct or memory.

Did Luke's death actually kill me too?

Not my body, but me. Me, here inside.

Well I'm not actually dead, I'm here deep inside.

I don't actually inhabit all of my body, I've retreated as far as I can get from the outside, a tiny ball within me.

No direct access to my energy, just here hibernating in the cocoon that was once me, like a foetus. What I see and hear is as if I'm watching, observing on a screen.

REALLY? MARLON?

Dear Marlon,

Are you really never going to tell me what happened?

You are the only one who knows what Luke's state of mind was
in his final hours of his life.
A life that was precious to me.
Are you really going to deprive me of that?
Of an account, however horrific?

Are you really going to let me suffer, strangled by my unanswered
questions?
Is there nothing left of the good that was once inside you?
Shame on you.
Silence is your admission of guilt.
You, and only you, choose that.

Luke's Mum

DO I NEED TO COMPLETELY
UNRAVEL TO REBUILD?

Oh fucking Saturday.
As a child, as a teenager, and in adulthood, Saturday was a day of joy, of family.

In this moment, it is a day of sadness, of reflection.
I wish more than anything that Luke was still alive, but more than that,
I wish Luke was alive and sober.

Is he sober now?
Is his spirit sober?
or does he remain in torment, seeking another state?
Is the state he's arrived in one where he's happy?
And if so, can I find peace in that?
Is my grief selfish?
Oh, how I'd like to talk to him now and find out.

If I had two minutes with him,
would I use that time wisely?
What would I say?
What would I do?
Would it ever be enough for me?
Am I the same as Luke, never enough?

Tonight I'll go to the Hollywood Bowl for the 1812 overture, where he went last year. I've always wanted to go but now in the loss of Luke, it brings me so little joy.

Bryan Adams wrote that well, 'Baby when you're gone, nothing feels or tastes like it should.'

Is the work I have to do, the thing to set Luke free?

That will need to be my driving force in the absence of anything else.
It's all there is.

lukelove.
Spread the lukelove.

Do I have to completely unravel in order to rebuild?

TURNING
TOWARDS LIFE

This week has shifted many sands. A connection with George, through his own despair, showed me that my inner "mother" is still available. There. My instincts awoken. In his troubles, the butterflies in my stomach were not just tangible, but they formed a new backbone to be there for him.

His loss of Luke, compounded with affairs of the heart, leave him at an impasse.
About to walk out the door, George arrived home sad and broken, lost.
Without hesitation I paused my own project and made myself available to him.

We talked about things that had previously been unvisitable.

About the torturous hours he sat in Denmark, mustering up the ability to call his Mother and Father, to break their world, their hearts, by telling them of their son's death. Luke's death. His brother's death.
Strangled by his own grief.

About how Luke's loss makes his mood in dealing with his other troubles twice as hard.

Where I had thought I had nothing to offer him as a mother, I saw that I did.
Where I thought I could not connect with him, I saw that I could.
I did.

We spent the afternoon together.
Talking.
Crying.
Laughing.
I dropped everything for this moment. Of course I did and I am glad that I did.
I am still of use to him.

Mindful that I was once told by a cousin that her mother was only happy when she was in crisis. I see that it's not that a mother is 'happy', but that she can see that she is of some use to her child, and that, to me, makes me feel of some worth.

A connection with your child is of such high value and often only required, tangible, when they are sad, sick, or at an impasse.

The connection is always there, but at this time when the subtle emotions are drowned out by the tsunami of loss, less sensed.

The luxury to take a moment and sit with your child,
when they want you,
is the most enriching reward.

Mothering, done properly, is and should be, thankless.
So, I am still of use.

I am thinking less of how my existence will damage George and more of how I can continue to be a good mother to him,
and in the way he needs me,
rather than how I need him to need me.

I am sad that George is sad.
It has been so hard to reach him because I have been locked in

my own bubble, unable to reach out, bobbing in my drifting emotional one-woman boat.

But it would appear that when the sharks swam in - I got my engine back and instinct drove me to his side.
And in that drive to help him, the connection helped me, probably more -
snapping me out of my self-obsessed misery and giving me the actual understanding that George needs me, rather than just hearing the repeated mantra from others over and over, "George needs you."
I couldn't feel it before,
knowing it or assuming is not enough.
Visceral knowledge, cellular knowledge, now restored - gives me energy, a call to arms - the road ahead becoming clearer.

The privilege of motherhood restored, the journey of commitment to my child, now a grown man, reforming in the light of new truths. George will need more and different support to navigate his new brotherless life. A real light now illuminates the path forward, together, in the terrible seas in which we live.

How to go on living with Luke's death as part of our story?

Being able to say the unsayable, while still remaining in life.
Adam too.

Issues in his life, in his trauma both before and in Luke's death.

Looking at the mess of our lives and striving to use this jolt of tragedy to catapult us all forward.
Almost using it for better.
Not wallowing.

Has George been afraid to lean on me?
afraid that the extra weight will harm me more than it will help him?
Afraid that I can take no more?
Have I feared the very same?

But in reality, George's leaning on my offered shoulder, is the making of me;
a restoration.

So who threw whom, the life jacket?

So again, I wonder if it is the same love that brought me to my knees, that will bring me to my feet.
A mother's love.

NEW LIFE BREATHED
INTO OUR FAMILY

Adam's lifetime project may be enacted.

All so interlinked, that we are all lifted by this.

Luke is punching the air. We all have new paths to follow.
All of us changed in losing Luke.

My positive energy seems to operate on a flywheel principle.

The more positive I feel.
The more positive I move.
The more positive I think.
The more I accept my new situation.
And so the more positive I feel.

The sense of healing rushes through me. A path forward is starting to form. The new opportunities seem good. It's almost 11 months since Luke died and somehow I feel closer to him than I have in a while.

As if his positivity has just been breathed into me.
And into Adam too.
And into George.
I am mindful that my friend Ian is flying in tonight and it may be this that I am looking forward to.
But for now I feel fortunate to have had Luke in my life for 23 years.
He's not forgotten and I will always love him and be sad that he is gone -

but how many of us get to experience lukelove?
Maybe it is lukelove that is coursing through my psyche?

I sang *Empire State of Mind* in the car on my way home this evening.
I felt him next to me - his energy on my fingertips as I reached out to him.

Grief is not linear, this I know,
so maybe this feeling will not last,
but I am grateful that I have it for now,
even if it may not stay.
I will enjoy it whilst it is here.

Complicated and brilliant to grieve,
whilst being happy that I ever had him,
and safe in the knowledge that on some level
I will always have him.

I date each page incorrectly.
It's as if I can't move
towards October
and
froze in July.

FROZEN

As Luke's yahrzeit, the anniversary of his death, approaches I realise that I do not move forward in mental date or time.

I see that at first I dated this page 302.
That's 30 days out.
And yes, although my mind is turning toward planning an event
to mark a year without Luke, my mind is in reverse, backing away
from the one year mark. It is not just a written error. As if on a
cellular level, I am unwilling to face the truth that my boy has
been dead for a year. On a cellular level I have frozen time.

The thoughts of suicide are shifting in the realisation that I did not
and do not want to kill myself - that is far too aggressive an act -
aggressive towards those who I leave behind, but simply that I
have not wanted to feel this way, to live this truth, and still don't.

The effort is so immense to walk towards recovery.
The effort to just exist in so much despair, too great.
The truth is, I just don't want to live in so much hurt.
The dream would be to just dissolve into my mattress one night
in an enchanted exit.
- not the dark and violent act of taking my own life.

The connection I experienced with George showed me that I am
of some value.
The work towards accepting a shitty fact like 'Luke is dead' - is
hardly anything to live for.
The connection I experienced with George, showed me something that is.

Thoughts still revolve around the details of Luke's death.
The final hours
the mood
was it fun?
an experiment?
or was he hurting?
Round and round and round.
The challenge to get Marlon to tell me.
Who else was present?
A dark hole that I feel the need to illuminate.
The trip to Boston, to see Marlon, is too dark and too heavy to make again.

Is it just a tantrum that I emotionally throw because I cannot have it?
Should I be building a tactical plan and long-term, patience-filled approach?
Should I just call him?
Should I write him a letter?
Should I involve his mother?
Yahrzeit approaching and I still don't know.

Luke didn't want to die.
He couldn't come back.
He would've if he could.

A yearning for his presence will get me nowhere.
A spiritual connecting is my only route.
Coupled with happy and true memories, his energy, his outlook.

I can learn from him now in the absence of dealing with his drug use.

Some of his friends still lost in their zombie states, filled with marijuana - the lost boys.

And so what of Luke?
Was he lost?
Was he lazy with his friend choice, choosing the wrong values over a more challenging friendship?
Drugs so normalised. Was weed the gateway?

They knew he took pills, but he defended his case, or went underground.
Did he just feel better with them in his system?
I have to admit that tonight I feel better with a heavy shot of vodka in me, and so I muse over what led Luke to take such drugs?
How did his decline, so steep, happen?
Yes, I know how it happens in others, but how in his?
Did I miss a trauma?
Was I a bad mother to him?
Should I have not stayed with an angry man?
How could such a lovely person be so carelessly lost to us all?

The risks he took - why can his friends not see that they, too, are taking such treacherous steps?
But whatever it was - I just want to put my arms around him and let him know how much I love him.

Oh, Luke! Wherever you are, I hope you know how much I love you.
Now and before your death.
It's not that I realise that now, in your absence - I knew it always.
The loss of you marks my soul now and forever,
the alter-definition of lukelove.

HIT OR MISS

Well, I'm still frozen in last month.
It's hard to explain how hit-or-miss my actions are.
If I succeed at anything at all; I feel like it's luck.
New tasks are not undertakable. I am stuck.

And to the eternal question inspired by the film *Arrival* -
If I could do it all over again? Would I?
To say that I would not feels disloyal to Luke and to my life
and so despite the pain I will not.

BUT
If I could change anything? What would I change?
Such a complicated question, but I think about this constantly.

There were chances and opportunities that I was so happy about,
thinking that they would be the making of him, I encouraged them
and yet they led to relapse.
There were times I was so glad that he had stopped hanging out
with certain friends only now to realise that the new ones brought
worse risks.
BUT
If those opportunities and new friends had not come along would
he have missed the opportunity to find his place in this world
where he was given such credit, a place where he was finally and
rightly proud of himself?
Were those things just incidental?
Was relapse a condition of his environment? Or was it inevitable?
Was his self-esteem separate or linked to relapse?
Luke's relapse right now takes center stage because although he
was so much more, it is what killed him.

If he'd had better people around him .... If....
and so it goes on round and round in my brain, haunting me.

I consider the Parable of the Chinese Farmer, illustrating how one
cannot predict whether any given event is for better or for worse.

I can see why religion would play its part here -
to believe there's a reason for everything
and to believe there's a reason for Luke's death.
To give one's self up to a higher power, accepting that we have no
influence over events.
A life without blame.

In the therapy of Luke's rehabs, parents are re-educated in parenting, to search for a new way, a way that helps their child, a way
to deal with the challenges their disease brings.
So IF I have no power over Luke's disease one way or another...
why the FUCK does my parenting matter?

In truth, I see a series of sliding doors,
chances missed, or not.
Things I could have said, or things I should have not.
A minute here, another day there ....
Would he still be alive?

I feel deeply responsible for Luke's death.
Despite what people tell me, I do blame myself,
and I search constantly, both consciously and subconsciously
for where I went wrong.

NOT JUST
MISSED BY HIS MUM

Dear Luke,

Today I am reminded of how amazing you were at your job.
You died whilst making *Wheelman*, and they have dedicated the movie to you.

I knew this was going to happen, my permission was sought, by the director, who took time to call me and tell me how incredible your on-set instincts were, how they sent you to do the tasks others could not, how you melted the darkness from grumpy performers and how, after your death, on one very challenging night, when everything was going wrong, he gathered the set to ask them to channel their inner Luke by asking themselves 'how would Luke have handled this?'.
And so the rest of that night's shoot went like a dream.

My pride is swelling, causing my heart to ache,
my tears to fall,
and the longing for another reality is re-awoken.

I miss you always,
but sometimes I am reminded of just how much I have lost,
and in parallel,
how lucky I am to have had anyone worth missing.
...........And not just missed by his Mum!

love Mum x

OPIOID AWARENESS DAY

The dedication to Luke on *Wheelman* is all over Luke's tribute page.
It reminds me of how he touched so many, so deeply.

My life feels like a mess. All of my failures are so all over me.
Losing you, the greatest failure of all.

I have no talents.
I have no career.
My body is a mess.
My youth is gone.
I have nothing to offer, especially now that my joy has gone.
I feel like I have made such a mess of everything, that I just want to give up and start again in the next life.

Oh, Luke,
this really took me down.

Was I so reliant on you for my worth?
Or is it that the loss of you made me feel powerless and nothing feels good in that light?

Somehow, tonight, this truth - the loss of you - isn't true.
I question everything and just want to bury myself in a hole.

LEAD BY EXAMPLE

An anniversary approaches - the last time I saw Luke alive.
I am lost. Deep in my sadness.

Wondering how I will ever be able to go on without Luke,
or is it how can I go on with the loss of Luke?

A medium told George that Luke said it is as hard for him to no longer be with us, as it is for us to no longer be with him. He misses being with us - the banter, the talk of tires..

This presents me with a strong motherly instinct to join him, or do I try and show him how to go on. Just as one overcomes a fear of spiders in order not to instill that fear in one's children, I'll overcome my inability to live in loss and show him how to proceed in this separation. We lead and so we show them the way.

Is this my journey? - to show Luke by example how to live apart?
Or live in parallel each on a side of mortality?

I remember that Luke would often call me Maman, in a French accent.
The memory of his enthusiasm in all things fills me like an infusion of all things that were good about Luke.
His zeal for life. His zeal for trying things new.
Experiencing all that the world has to offer.

This is also what killed him.

HOW DO I PROCEED?

In continuation of a thought,
Luke is on his own.
Separated on the other side of mortality.

The draw to join him is still so strong - he doesn't like to be alone.

The strong pull towards him was tangible at equine therapy.
Adam has George and Luke is alone.

Can I show Luke how to move forward in this ghastly separation,
from this side of mortality? - By my example? What does that look
like?

Does it dishonour Luke's life, his memory, to move on?
Or is to move on the honour I give him?
Move on in his name?
In my work?
In helping others?
Somehow?
OR
Is it his joy of life that shows me how to move on?

Children teach you as much as you teach them.
They mould you as much as you mould them.
This delicate dance, now interrupted by Luke's death, is confusing,
and yet is still happening.

Selecting photos for his Yahrzeit, a record of a childhood, a life
with Luke.
In some photos I see the change in his eyes.

Is it adolescence or something more sinister?

If I move forward will it help him too?
Or shall I suspend the rest of my life, as if holding my breath?

George's upset, has certainly offered me a drawbridge towards him.
Was that what was hard for him?
To lean on a broken parent?
And in doing so, did he think it selfish - that it would tip me?

But that was not what happened - it was, for me, a joining up with the living.
Is that a message to siblings left behind?

We want to be close to all our children.
Grief draws us towards our lost children, numbs us from the love of our living children.

Oh, to find a way to be with them both, not to make the Sophie's Choice.

MAGIC FEATHER

It's a year today that Luke left for Boston. It's the last time I kissed him, hugged him, touched him, breathed him in.
Smelled the scent that he was born with - still recognizable under the smell of cigarettes. The personal scent that, even blindfolded, I would recognise, anywhere.

I left him with the customary
I love yous
Have funs
Drive safes

I hugged him and left for my appointment.
The partings of a mother and son.
I was happy for him.
A new chapter in his life.

As I drove away I texted: "Send me a photo so I can remember what you look like."
He did.

Had I stayed, would I have had another hour, another five minutes, another...
Would it have made a difference?
Would it ever have been enough?

We were both excited about his new project, a feature film with a crew out of area. Shrewd career move. A plan setting a foundation for the future, for when he made the Directors Guild. For when he was a 2nd Assistant Director. So that he would have contacts and colleagues for "out-of-area" days.

"Send me a photo so I can remember what you look like."

He wanted feature films on his resumé, and he wanted to go far.
How proud I was.
This was not a boy without purpose.
He loved his job and his job loved him.
He seized the opportunity that was given to him.
Found a free place to stay (with a friend from the past; Marlon),
and was off to drive across the USA to do so, in the car that he
prized and paid for.

This is not the substance abuser that you can spot.

The photo he sent shows clear skin, shiny hair, wit and ambition.

He had humour, sharp instincts, and planning skills.
An excellent P.A.
A man going places.

So what did I miss?
What should I have seen, that I did not?

In the past months I have wondered and searched my soul -
Did I fight hard enough for him?
Where did I fail him?

Memories of Boston when George was insistent that it was not
drugs that killed Luke.

"He knew what he was doing."
"He was just having fun, Mum."

I turned on George like a rabid dog.
"Do you think he's having fun now?"

My response was so visceral, so violent. So angry at the notion that drug use is not deadly - even in the face of Luke's death. And yet it takes so long for verification. The delays of toxicology reports and autopsies unimaginably long at 3-6 months. Often longer.

The truth is:
Drugs are fun, ...until they are not.
Drugs work, ...until they don't.
And yet, as Luke's mother - an educated woman, aware of his penchant for drug use -
I had no fucking idea... that he was in the grip of opioid use.

I would later read in the texts on his phone that he and Marlon had planned a drug binge.

As I stood there and said goodbye, so much pride and excitement for Luke's career-move and planning for the future, I had no idea that he had also planned a drug-fuelled fest in Boston.

Three weeks later, he would be dead.
And I had no idea!
What kind of mother am I?

High functioning and full of dreams and concrete plans, he left for Boston and never returned - just a wooden box of ashes, in which his hair would not have fit.

Yes he liked to smoke weed.
Yes he loved to party.
Yes, the thresholds were high.
But coupled with steady employment, constant job offers, and plans that were materializing for a successful future of great

things…

How could I know that underneath, his body was dealing with so much abuse?

What did I miss that set him apart from the other 23-year-old boys with exciting lives, and glittering futures - that was not to be?

What can I learn from this?
What advice can I pass to others?

In life, after an episode, Luke would later explain what went wrong, what I had spotted but not fully added up.

He would show me.

Now his phone documents, through text messages and maybe more apps that I have yet to find - a map of how this magical boy, still able and functioning on a level higher than most could ever wish to attain, fell to heroin via pharmaceuticals of many kinds. The drugs didn't halt him - it appears, until his death, that they made his life easier.

In an age of instant gratification,
There's a pill to wake you up.
There's a pill to allow you to sleep.
There's a pill to take away pain.
A pill to enable you to function in a world where much is demanded of you, in order to perform and achieve greatness - which indeed he did.
The proof is clear.
He was a great worker.
A unicorn, in fact.

Was it the drugs that enhanced his abilities to such great heights? And if so, in his enormous pride of his abilities to please and to perform so well, as he did - did he think, or know, that none of this was possible without them?

Was Luke a high-functioning person *because* of the drugs and not *despite* them?

Were they, to him, as the magic feather was to Dumbo?

Far from the stereotypical junkie.

We live in a world where performance-enhancing drugs are commonplace. Sportsmen have reported in their droves that they cannot be competitive in a field where others are using performance enhancers.

Antidepressants keep the school carpools on track for many.
Pain relievers keep the masses fully employed and away from bed rest.
Diseases are kept in remission.
Is it, in concept, all the same?

With Luke's ADD, I have asked many psychotherapists - why Strattera and not weed?

For a time it would appear, that the drugs did work.
What I have to live with now, is that in the end, ...they did not.
They killed him.
But 'til that happened, they clearly did work.

Everyone's involved in this opioid crisis, in this world of heightened performance.

The drug companies requiring more sales.
The Xalisco boy's pride in paying for quinceañeras back home.
People shut off from effective holistic healthcare.
People trying to stay employed to feed their families.
Politicians going for the popular vote, for the funding.

....All victims of the honourable olympic tenet.
Faster, higher, stronger.
Is this the true root of the crisis of our time?

In the movie *The Crash Reel*, which documents the life of the great snowboarder Kevin Pearce, after an awful head trauma, his life, his personality, his ability, changed, forever, Kevin's mother speaks, as if to me personally, about how even we, the mums, and not just the sponsors and teams, are guilty of causing this drive for bigger and better tricks - They land a double and immediately set their sights on a triple. Us too.

At the time, I heard it as another snowboard mum. But now, I hear it, albeit too late,
as an ordinary mum.
As Luke's mum. (Although being Luke's mum has always been far from ordinary.)

If one's child just lies in bed, plays Xbox, or stays at home - no job, no friends - we are angst-ridden, and often we are angry. We want an achieving kid, and even if we don't, the child thinks we do. That's where all the praise is.

If that child struggles to face the world naked, but wants societal praise, does it not seem reasonable to take a performance-enhancing drug?
'Dutch Courage' - that sip of wine, or gin and tonic, that separates

us from our worries and gives us some back-bone or eases the day - performance enhancing.

The antidepressant, so we can get out of bed or improve our entrance into a boardroom - performance enhancer.

Look how proud I was of Luke's achievements.
Look how I glowed with pride.
Look how I encouraged it.
Look at how Luke and I praised George for the viral Instagram post of his Miller flip - it's all in our last texts.
Are we all encouraging this international drug problem?

All of us, at one moment in time, need a performance enhancer of some sort in order to face the world.

Looking down at myself right now.
Sitting in 'The Stoge garden' outside Luke's room
headphones on, music that connects me to Luke blaring insanely loud in my ears,
chain smoking cigarettes,
drinking tea.
It's 12:27 PM.
I have eaten nothing.
I am not showered, nor dressed.
I've not brushed my teeth.
I've not brushed my hair in days.
I don't care.
I am sobbing.
My robe is drenched in my flowing tears.
My legs are tracked with the salt of dried tears.
My eyes are swollen and crusted from expelling those tears.
Deep in my grief.

The song *Pump It Louder* in my ears now, so loud I am sure to damage my hearing.

My life at a standstill.

If you could see me now, would you think I need a pill?

This is grief.

Raw, hard, consuming.

Naked, unmasked, uncomfortable.

A mother tortured by the loss of her child.

Some are not so lucky. "*Let's Get It Started*" blares in my ears and I can't get it loud enough. I will purge this wave of emotions and process my thoughts and in a few hours I will be through this moment, for now, but to the outside world, would I look like I am not functioning?

Was Luke not afforded this luxury?

IT'S A LOVE SONG

Adam says "But Sheila, it's a love song".
It is true; the music that I am using to express my grief is mostly love songs.

Songs of longing, missing, desperate loss.
These are love songs.
I love Luke. I miss Luke. I ache for Luke.
"I want you so bad it's my only wish."
"I am right at the borderline."
I am looking out for Luke, night and day.
My heart IS pushed to the limit.
Can you meet me halfway, Luke?

I played this Black Eyed Peas song when Luke was in Wilderness.
It was the CD in our car.
I'd sing it and cry, loud.
As if I could reach him far away in Utah.
I extend this now to the other side of mortality.
It's the perfect anthem for me right now, as it was then.

Love is love.
But mother-child love is the most epic of them all.

Tears roll across my limbs as they fall from my face.

MY WAY FORWARD

It's 2.30 am.

Rattling about, no wish to sleep.

Vodka at my side, a cigarette in one hand, pen in the other...

Grief Group tonight showed me how many forms of grief and routes forward there are.

People stuck in a maze of anger at the people who surround them.

People stunned into shock, manifesting in physical disability - just one too many blows to their nervous system.

People still in the early stages of weeping and agony.

People with broken marriages, friendships, connections with life and love and incompetent strangers.

People with stigma toward substance abuse death; apparent, institutionalised.

No harm meant, but there, even in the safe haven of a grief group that is steadily filling up with substance disorder deaths, mostly heroin, the stigma is harbored.

I realised today that the way forward seems clear to ME, for now.

Not so that I can describe it -

but that I know I am on it.

A REINTERPRETATION
OF OUR MORAL CODE

My friend is here. Rather a particular friend.
In my endeavour not to blame others for Luke's death, the eternal quest to balance my thoughts -
That when drugs are involved - shit happens.
In the world of drug use, Luke may just as easily have been the hand that took another's life.

Another reminds me that, all said and done, Luke would never have left a mother alone in a beach house on the other coast of America and not shown up to explain the events, whether or not he had promised to come.

I am cautious with this.
For years, I have watched bereaved parents on TV describe their lost children as the most happy, loving, caring, perfect beings.
Do only the perfect die?
Why do they not describe their imperfections, in balance?

So I do allow myself to think, what I suspect to be true - that Luke would likely stand honourably before the grieving mother and answer, as best he could, the questions that burn her heart.

Was he truly so different from others caught in the same scenario?
In truth, I think he was.

He was far from perfect, that's what made him special.
But I would have supported him to do what is right, even after doing what was wrong.

Or would he never had let her come, rather than leave her hanging?
Or am I, too, a mother in denial?
Or had he just not reached that point, yet?

I am shaken by my friend - a realist - a friend of truth.
Whatever the truth may have been, I am touched by her accidental eulogy for Luke.

Substance use leaves so much destruction in its wake.
A deserted battlefield filled with unmapped land mines, unexploded shells, pot holes, residual anthrax, just under the soil - no clue of their location.

Are there people who have died from Luke's deadly offerings, that neither he nor I know of?

Drugs set a ruleless playing field with a reinterpretation of our moral code, where 'helping a friend' may kill them.
Where offering people more fun can blind and maim.

Luke would harm no one intentionally, but drugs create a world of bad ideas, however well-intentioned. Judgment impairment is both the goal and the abhorrent side effect.

Luke would have struggled to cope with what Marlon faces.

Millions do not come to sobriety because of such events.
Millions do not step up honourably.
Baffling.

A NOTE ON THE INTENTIONS
OF SUBSTANCE ABUSE

As I wrestle with the vocabulary for the condition that Luke was in - the redefining of words like junkie, addict, abuse...

I remind you now -
No child grows up planning to be a drug addict.
It's not the plan.
It's not an aspiration.
Somehow, it just happens, and the roads to that place seem to be as numerous as those who find themselves there, whether they know it or not.

I know Luke did not plan this.

I don't know if he had a brain disorder, a genetic susceptibility or whether he was just experimenting, having fun.

Science has theories, no one has a theory to fit all.

So much money is being made on the "cures" and "treatments". No one cure to fit all.

The FDA blocks Ibogaine, an addiction interrupter.
States argue about access to Naloxone, Suboxone.

AA and NA have a system that speaks to some, and yet not to others.

Some nations have full decriminalisation.
Some are raging a war on drugs.

Perceptions shift.
Normalisation of drug use is widespread.
Stigma is alive and well.
Rappers glorify it.

All I can say is that the road to where I am now is as unbearable
as the arrival.

Whether you are in the midst of your own or your child's drug
use, my heart goes out to you and I wish I could make it better.

So I lay my pebble at the foot of your unfathomable mountain and
tell you -
You are not alone.
And I send you love, support, and empathy.
and the greatest, most optimistic gift of all;
lukelove.

And the tears fall once more.

TEARS

Where do all these tears come from?
More powerful than opium.
An endless supply.
They are my constant companion.
My strength and my weakness.

To those who walk in my shoes:
Cry for your lost babies.
Scream their names.
Light your candles.
Tattoo your skins.
Love them in death as you did in life.
Carry on - or don't.
Hang with their friends and yours, or shut yourself away.
Talk or be silent.
Function or not.
Go to action or lie in bed.

I characteristically do it all at once.
But I'll not tell you that this isn't hell.

NOLUKE, NO NOTHING.
NO FILTER

Well, it's actually day 345 at 1am.
My eyes are dry, itchy, swollen, from the outpourings of the past
three days.

I am still.
Still inside.
Restless - not wanting to go to bed.

I am so nicotine-ridden that I can hardly smoke - but I still do.
No sense of Luke about to come home, or call, or anything.
The stillness is the death of hope, the death of denial,
the death of aspiration of what may have been.

Wondering if this is the dreaded second year mark looming. They
say it's the worst.

I miss my dance partner.
I miss my powerhouse of energy.
I miss his smile.
His laugh.
I am just dead inside.
Feet on the ground.
No tears.
Just still.
Exhausted.
Existing!

DON'T GET STUCK
IN "LOSS"

Someone writes to me today, "Don't get stuck in loss, it's a waste of a life."
I know this email is well-meant. But it makes me furious.

This person is my former therapist.
She's smart,
she's brilliant,
she's a recovered addict,
as is the friend who will have reported his findings to her after our visit.

But this email has my blood boiling.
This loss is so deep and so layered, so nuanced - how can I not get lost in it?
Maybe lost to them, lost to the outside world, but I am not lost, I am in here, in my grief, working intensely.
If I was not working the grief, I would be stuck.
I'd look OK from the outside, but I would be nowhere, I'd just be denying the questions, the dilemma, the guilt, the 'shoulda woulda couldas'.

This is not the loss of a lover, a parent, this is a deeper loss.
The loss of a child
The loss of MY child
The loss of Luke.
The loss of confidence in my parenting.
The loss of identity.
The loss of aspiration for Luke.
The loss of a future.

When I lost Luke I lost a battle, long fought.

There's a lot of advice to be given, it would appear, and my instant retort would be:

"Until you have walked in my shoes..."

But many have. And many will.

The advice I receive by way of those who share in my grief group, who have walked in these heavy shoes, still does not always apply.

So I will quote Luke:

"If it doesn't apply... ...let it fly."

But this well intentioned advice enrages me, and so, I am curious to know why.

Although I remain sad, sometimes bereft -

I am not, I feel, stuck.

Grieving is exhausting.

But grieving is what I am doing.

The process for me has many different channels, like a multicore cable.

There's the **detective**.

Who searches through Luke's phone and talks to his friends, for clues about his state of mind - where he was with his drug use.

Which friends are enabling?

Which are not?

Who else is in danger?

Is George in danger?

How the events that lead to his death unfolded?

The **activist**.

Where the drugs came from?

Who should be shut down?
How to help halt this terrible epidemic?
What can I do to help?
The reaching out to others.

The **mother**.
Who has lost a son.
A companion.
A dance partner.
Who failed to protect.
Who tried so hard.

The **human**.
Struggling to go forward in loss of identity.
The loss of her war on drugs.

The **mother of George**.
How can I help him?
How can I be better for him?
Suffering in his suffering.

The **spiritualist**.
Listening out for Luke.
Enjoying what I can of him, divided as we are by mortality.

The **survivor**.
Who sometimes does not want to survive.
And equally, ...sometimes does.
Both -
In the name of Luke's memory, and in defiance of heroin and this
disorder of substance abuse.
To lead by example.

The **exhausted** human.
Worn down by the mud in which I swim.
Haunted by Luke's journey and his last minutes, hours, days, weeks on this earth.

The **administrator**.
Planning suitable remembrances, tributes, and setting a tone that suits both those here, surviving Luke, and Luke himself.

These versions are all me. **ALL me**.

Sometimes I am one of them, sometimes I am all of them at once.
A corporation within me, of Sheilas, who serve in different roles.
I am still understaffed it would seem.
Creative Sheila is a little overwhelmed by the others, friend-of-others Sheila is too.

Hedonistic Sheila has had her power cut, or has she lost a vital part of her department in her inability to connect with others?
So am I really stuck?

As I process and examine all of these elements?

I exercise three times a week.
I go to therapy.
I am working on a book.
I am counselling another mum with a child lost in his substance use.
I am assisting in writing a script. In fact three scripts.
I plan and hold social events for Luke's birthday and anniversary of his death so that we may share with others our loss and their's?
I get dressed (most days).
I shower.

I swim.

I brush my teeth (mostly)

I eat.

I do some chores.

I smoke a lot of cigarettes.

And, above all, I continue to look into myself to examine why and how it is I feel this way.

And it's dark.

If I was jolly, and back out there working, socialising, and rushing about, I would not actually be functioning, but merely appearing to do so.

I would be ignoring my internal turmoil.

I would not be working through my grief.

I would be bypassing it.

That may be easier for others to witness. But in truth, for me, the grief would still be there, like an unopened parcel full of hats to wear.

As I try each hat on (and often wear them all together) I work through all the viewpoints and experiment with what feels best to me. What works, what do I see, what do I feel?

Maybe what makes my blood boil is that my friend's account to this woman was false, undimensional, and the sadness that accompanies such a lazy observation from someone whom once I dug so deep to understand and help. Change of hat: but maybe he does not have my tools? So how could he?

Hat of Forgiveness.

Hat of Understanding - that some have limitations.

Hat of Revenge.

Hat of Police.

Hat of an addict.
Hat of Marlon.
Hat of a dealer.
Hat of Big Pharma.
Hat of a politician.
Hat of Luke's friends.
Hat of Adam.
Hat of George.
Hat of Luke. There's sometimes various hats of Luke.
Hat of Mother.

In early recovery, from the outside, it appears as though the person just concentrates on one thing. That may be how it appears, but in my wisdom, I know that isn't true.

It's not true of me either.

GEORGE

George is the only one of us who has not known a life without Luke.

As we select photos for the anniversary video, we see a documentation of our life in images.
Adam and I.
Me pregnant.
Luke's scan.
Luke's arrival.
Luke's first two years.
And George, now swelling in my belly.
Then George.

Through the 20 years, they sit together - always.
They have a visible bond.
There was, for George, no life without Luke.

And at a time of great need, his parents are all fucked up too!!!!

Christ! How can George's grief ever be considered anything but the most disorienting?

Why is sibling grief so overlooked?

WHY? HOW?

We never found out why Luke turned to drugs.
We found no trauma in all of his therapy, nothing was identified.
This doesn't mean there was none, simply that I, at least, know of
none.

The search for a gene has been fruitless so far.
Is it genetic?
Is it hereditary?
Or are we looking in the wrong place?

In my emotional travels, the work of Brian L. Weiss, MD in *Many
Lives, Many Masters*, has brought a suggestion to my soul-seek-
ing.
He tells of his discovery of patients with untreatable trauma. In
sessions, the clients regress into past lives and there he treats
their trauma with miraculous outcome.
The past life trauma could not be treated in this life, unless they
regressed to the life in which it was inflicted.

How do these traumas transport from one life to another?
Is the trauma carried in the soul?

Was that Luke?
Was that where his trauma lay?
Is the 'gene' for addiction... actually, on the soul?

Is that what happened to Luke?
Was that where his trauma lay?
On his soul?
Was his trauma not from this life?

171

Was that trauma what triggered his drug-fuelled escape?

Is the 'gene' for addiction in fact, on the soul?

What needs to be completed in this life that could not be completed in the last?

NIGHT

So muddled is my head with the unsettled thoughts of Luke's death.

I went to bed in a timely fashion. I was sleepy. So I went to bed at the same time as Adam and George, remembering the comfort of my soft bed, like a cloud-like nest that felt so good this morning. I relished that thought and went there. But I was not met with that comfort. I did not drift into sleep. Instead my bed is a stone, pushing at my bones, my head whirs with a jumble of soundbites.
George's fateful words, "Luke is gone. Luke is dead."
Unachieved and imagined conversations with Marlon.
What I want to say to him, what I imagine him to reply.
Where is Luke? Is he okay?
Thoughts of his halted breath.
My heart beats now, strong and tangible. My stomach gurgling.
Flashbacks of the past 11 months... and before.
My last words with Luke.
My encounters since.
Sentences - what I have heard, what I have said.
What I will never have an opportunity to say.
Composing letters to Marlon.
Phone calls, texts.
It's rushing at me all at once, in a sequence of sound clips.
Some loud, and some soft.
Overlapping, confused.
The unfinished quest to find out what happened, what I missed, how it could have been different.

How I will go forward?
Up and down to the bathroom.

Thirst.

Constipation.

The undigestible facts and imaginings that make up my life now.

This is why I don't go to bed until I am exhausted.

This is why I wait until I have nothing left before I hit my bed.

This is why I watch TV and play mindless games on my iPad and phone, to block out the noise of my unfinished work -

The puzzle of what led my boy to his death, and the part those around him played in that. The part I played.

I have been productive the past few days.

I have done a job, I did it well.

The challenge of an all-night calligraphy stint, the 'to-ings and fro-ings' of all the client changes and corrections and all met as if Luke had never died. As if my heart had never been broken.

I took a trip to the flower market and designed the centrepiece for Luke's Yahrzeit as I would have before.

And now, here I am at 2:00 AM, sleepless, with all the thoughts that would have streamed across my mind (had they not been blocked) for the past four days - rushing at me all at once. Four days of this awful nightmare condensed into now.

A slot machine of images, questions, and imagined solutions, replies.

Where cherries or bells would present.

It won't quiet, and although they were clear as I lay in bed, not finding sleep, now that I have risen to flush them onto this page - they fade like a dream upon waking, and I can neither fix them nor identify them, though the confusion that they bring still swirls in every cell of my being.

The police - yes, I must call them and ask:

Why did they not call us themselves?

Did Marlon block them?
What was the alcohol swab on the nightstand for?
How was the heroin administered?
What did that scene look like?

Should I go back to Boston?
Should I hire a private investigator?

The women who warned of the opioid crisis early on; ignored as frazzled bereaved women. Why is this in the U.K. press, and less in the U.S. press?
The women from the documentary *Heroin(e)* so valiantly working to save people.
The line, "Taking heroin is like kissing Jesus."
How does it feel to suffocate into heroin?
Is Luke okay?
What can I do for him?
Is George okay?
What can I do for him?
When I die, will I reunite with Luke?
What have I forgotten to do?
Should I do a juice cleanse?
Where are my floristry scissors?
Round and round and back to my never-had conversations with Marlon and how to reach into him so he will tell me - the letters I plan to write.

It's almost a year and yet my puzzle is far from completed.
It's clear that my fight for the answers is far from over.

My quest for the truth is clear, but how will I intertwine my life with this?
How can I have another life in parallel whilst I do this?

And where is Marshall?

Is he safe?

How can I help in this awful world where drugs are normalised?

And when the drugs are becoming increasingly hazardous with Fentanyl-laced MDMA and cocaine, killing even the most casual of party users.

Where is my place in this?

How do I clear this awful disease of the stigma it carries?

It's clear that returning to 'normal' life as it was before Luke died will not serve me long-term. Not yet.

This dark and painful world is where I live now.

Only in doing some good will I avenge the evil of addiction and drug abuse.

The question is, can I find a new approach?

A new way in - a way that works.

NEW HAT. NEW VOICE

Can't use a ballpoint pen. Must use a pencil - not because my words cannot be indelible - but because the lightness of a pencil in hand is required to slip my thoughts through. Yes girl, "write that shit down." It's gilded on the side of this pencil.

I am not stuck in loss, but investigating all of the openings that this space has afforded my mind.

Open to things.
Open to everything.
Open to a new channel.
Free under the awning of grief to explore what has, to me, been unexplorable.
New angles on what brings people to destroy themselves.
Coming in on a tangent that may be considered unacceptable.
To go forward I must cast out doubts set in me by the judgment of others.
Doubts set there by societal norms.
Scars inflicted by school-appointed experts.
"You are not a good writer."
"You know nothing about addiction because you are not an addict."
"That's not based on science."
"You are not a therapist."
"You are too idealistic."
"That's not the real world."
"This has been happening for centuries."
So letting through the words of those who spoke to me from outside the formal boundaries of judgment..... Let's hear those voices.
"Oh my God you have a way with words!"

"You write so beautifully!"

"You should write!"

"I have come to realise that you are just waiting for the rest of us to catch up."

The concept of a reality TV show to be called; *Sheila gets it done*!

"I came to you because I needed someone who would sort it out, get it done"

"If she says she'll do it - She will".

In my reply to my apology, when I am proceeding on a project in chaos,

"I am just going to do it the girl way." (On vision rather than prep.)

Luke would reply,

"What you mean is, you're actually doing it, rather than just talking about it."

So here's my conundrum.

When I speak, my voice is too strong to digest.

Too opinionated?

Too raw?

Too much truth?

How do I get people to hear me long enough to consider what I say?

The written word? rather than the spoken word?

I process as I speak - this is a truth.

Do the pencil and paper filter some of the space between me and the receiver, and give them time to colour in what I say in a digestible form?

Or, does my position as a grieving mother, my pride of Luke, my honesty, my sadness, my forgiveness, my fragility, bring with it a light that inspires rather than threatens?

What is true is that all the experts in the world have not found a solution to the issue of drug use - a way of bringing people universally out of self-destruction.

Money drives the business of supply, and the business of rehabilitation - but does it detract from common sense?
Do liability issues scare the FDA from exploring Ibogaine?
Or is there not enough money to be made?
Does the climate of our times inhibit us from allowing common sense to prevail?
How can trying Ibogaine be any more dangerous than heroin or meth?
A five-year-old can see it's worth a shot.
The grown-up world calls in all the reasons against it, but does it make it right?
Does it make it the course to follow? - NO!

People feel brow-beaten by the establishment. They feel powerless.
We see that apathy in the low voting figures. "Why bother, all politicians are the same?".
And indeed, in this matter, it is true.

Wake up it's time to look deep
Open your mind and see.
Shine the light and see.
God bless, you, Tinchy Stryder for those words.

So my mind is open.
Luke's was too.
I may not have the answer, but if I do nothing, then nothing will come of it - but do I dare to try?

The other way does not work for millions.

I'll ask questions, I'll play with ideas - time for a new way.

Nothing will change if we think nothing will change.

Time for me to find a new tone to my voice so it will be heard, but without adjusting the message, to fit into a constraint that restricts the actions.

The quest for knowledge and change.

The unanswered questions that lock Luke's death in lies.

The dimensions around us, and how to channel them.

The way forward to lead an entire generation away from destruction.

The new place for me and my family in a world without Luke in bodily form.

The opening of my heart and mind so that I may find peace and a way to help others in my recovery.

A way to make something good out of the world's loss of my magical Luke, of all the world's magical lost children.

A PITEOUS SOUND

Alone in the house I am sobbing. Small howls of despair. A piteous sound.

I've become intrigued about the act of crying.
What is it for?
Where does this come from?

I found an article on the world wide web that talks of how crying is an alert to those around us that we need comfort.
But I am alone - as I mostly am when I cry - and even in company I wave off the assistance of others, as there is nothing they can do.

It's true that tears are a painkiller, a sedative. More soothing than opium, that drain into your nose and down your throat.
God knows I need that.
But what is the display, the noise?
Am I crying for Luke?
Am I crying for me?
Am I crying to Luke?

As I write my thank you email to the director of *Wheelman* for his dedication, on the film Luke didn't quite finish - (Only death would stop Luke from following through), I cry, I weep. Is this display for myself? Is this a yielding to honour my sadness, my loss? Does it make me feel lonely to cry in solitude? My grief is lonely. Grief is lonely.
Although so many are sad, so many mourn the loss of Luke - are we in the end all alone in our personal loss of Luke?
In Luke's life are we each privy to a personalised relationship with

him, an experience so individual, so private to each and every one of us - that the loss of him, is too, just as personal, just as individual, just as private.

Is the saying "We all grieve in our own way" the counterbalance, or expression, of our own particular relationship with that person in life?
So still I sit here, alone and crying.
Am I hoping that somehow it will bring him back?

Or is it like praying?
Am I demonstrating devotion?
A display that I miss him and am bereft without him? Because that is true.
No anger.
No resolve to change the world.
No drive for truth today.
Just sadness.

I now feed off people with
hearts full of love
That keep me afloat
'til I find my new self

DO WE NOT UNDERSTAND
'TIL IT HAPPENS TO US?

Sitting, reading, deep in the mysteries of the opioid crisis.
Articles replying to the "Where were their mothers?"
They were right fucking there!
Thousands and thousands of us. Millions of us.

The Guardian newspaper, an article about the fight that started
12 years ago.
Challenges to the FDA, senators, pharmaceutical companies, doctors, they wrote, they banged on doors.
They are intelligent, clear. They are well researched.
They are part of an army of mothers, active, vibrant, brilliant.
I am in awe.
The heroines of our age.
Yet they were dismissed.

I am overwhelmed by the hopelessness of this situation.
I cannot see how these women could have done more.
I cannot see how *I* could do better.
The power of money, of profit, of lobbying, is so powerful.

Should we just lie down and allow this epidemic to continue to
take our children?
It's so hard to explain the myriad components, as varied as they
are numerous, that bring so many to their deaths.
The numbers so vast.
21 million Americans suffer from substance use disorder.
On average, 175 people die EVERY DAY.
1 in 3 families are affected
and yet....

The stigma still so strong, so pervasive.

This is not happening to other people any longer - it is happening to you.

Odds are, if you think it isn't, you just haven't realised, yet.

The work, the blogs, the Facebook groups of mothers in grief, in political reform, supporting those whose children are in active addiction.

What could I possibly add?

How can I make a difference?

Where would my energy be best placed?

What new angle can I take?

What would make a difference?

The grip of the mighty dollar around the throats of those who could.

The FDA protects Pharma.

So much money involved in the legal lobbying of government, of the FDA.

How can we ever go up against that and win?

The FDA - who are they? What is their designated role?

"Pharma has a right to make money", they say.

The human cost to the nation does not appear to be of their concern, their duty.

Do the American people know this?

Do they understand how this works?

If it's approved, do they presume that 'facts' have been checked, the studies, the trials?

Do they understand, know, that the criteria for a drug trial are often posthumously altered by the FDA so that the new drugs can be passed into approval?

And what could they do about it, even if they knew?

Is it corruption?

Or is it just the way things work?

A form of anarchy, with shifting rules and regulations to enable large companies to ever increase profit?

Is it too overwhelming?

Is this powerlessness part of the quest to numb our senses?

Our sensibilities?

Is everything so far out of control, so far from human consideration, that those who stand up for change will just become exhausted and fade?

Will I ?

Is the stigma of drug abuse at the root of this apathy?

Is substance abuse more stigmatised than greed?

Is Greed, one of the seven deadly sins, now considered above human life?

Not just Luke's life, but millions of lives.

How many people must die at that altar before it changes?

These women, so brilliant, so numerous, doing such good work - but in the end, are we all just preaching to the choir?

Do we not care until it happens to us?

Do we not understand it until it happens to us?

Feeling hopeless.

IS IT STILL TRUE?

The anniversary of the loss of Luke is looming.
A countdown to his death, offset by a year.

Today, 365 days ago, is the last time we spoke.
The images of what he was doing this time a year ago pass through me, like watching him die, unable to do anything, helpless now as we were then.
It's harder and harder to function.
I've spent days in bed.
I've spent days being productive, preparing for the day of his remembrance.
I am unhinged.
I am anxious.
The panic attacks lurk just under my skin, ready to take me over.

I chew my nails,
I twirl my hair
My eyes are swollen from weeping.
I am nauseous.
My appetite is scant.
I buy tickets for the cinema for the wrong day.
I am distracted.

I tried to look for a new handbag today, a kindly friend in tow.
It's hard to concentrate on wanting anything whilst staying true to myself - what I like, what my needs are when, in truth, all I truly want is to have Luke back.
For me.
For Adam.
For George.

Our project to honour Luke's memory keeps us moving.

Buttons designed and ordered.

Food ordered.

Adam is making a candle, formed from the leftovers from all the candles we have burned every night for the past year.

We do what we can - we try to create beauty in his memory.

We try to find beauty to honour him.

But the loss is overwhelming.

My lovely Luke.

My dance partner.

My advisor.

My adversary.

My charge.

My firstborn.

...is gone.

And yet I still cannot believe it to be true.

How can I mourn so deeply when all at once, I don't truly believe it to be true.

All the candles, tattoos, buttons, flower arrangements, as if, on some level, it will bring him back to life.

Back to me.

COUNTDOWN

It is 12:27 AM.

The countdown to the loss of Luke makes me numb, as if the reality of his death eludes me. Leaving me sleepless, staying up late, waiting for him as I did the past 25 years.

This time, 25 years ago, I was pregnant. His tiny form already growing in my womb.

The countdown began then.

The countdown to his first kick.

The countdown to a peek of him on a scan.

The countdown to his birth.

The myriad countdowns that are part of mothering.

First words.

First steps.

First day at school.

First meeting of his baby brother.

The endless countdowns of his equestrian life.

The show jumping rounds.

The safe return from cross-country courses.

That beaming smile I would see from afar, if all had gone well, or, the fury on that same face if it had not.

The countdown to the final whistle on the football fields.

The countdown to exams.

The countdown to their results.

The countdown to going on holiday.

The countdown 'til dinner was ready.

The countdown to Christmas.

And then the drugs appeared, bringing new countdowns.

The countdown 'til he was released from Wilderness.
The countdown on the endless plane journey for his graduation
ceremony.
The countless flights to and from therapeutic boarding school.
The long drives with and without him to and fro.
To visit him.
To take him for a lunch, a day, a week.
To return him.
The family always separated by miles. By time zones.

The countdown 'til we were all together.
The countdown of days clean.
The countdown 'til he was home from work.
And now the only countdowns in my heart... are.

The countdown to the anniversary of his death and
The countdown to my own death, so that we may once again be
reunited.
Together, to hold him as I did at his birth.

No notion of a countdown 'til I'm happy in life.
A mother is always happiest when her family is all around her.
Well I was. "When the boys are both home."
No more is that to be, for me.

My family are coming for Luke's remembrance day.
I wish there was a happier reason for the gathering.

I wish I was arguing with Luke right now
about giving up his room for my Mum, in exchange for
the sofa.
I wish he could be here.

WHY CAN'T HE
NOT BE DEAD?

It was a Friday that I was last happy.
Luke's last day alive was a Friday. Friday the 30th of September.

The day and the date are offset because it is another year on
and so the "lasts" are spread over 48 hours.
For the first time the confusion of time zones, days, dates may
seem like a blessing.
The exact moment of Luke's death will never be mine to know.

Would it be worse to know?
Would it be a second in time that would arrive and fleetingly pass?
Is this drawn out "last" easier to bear exactly because I do not
know?

For the past 11 months and 28 days I have obsessed about knowing.
So as this Friday bleeds into Saturday and inevitably into the date
of his death,
I am thinking only of what I can only imagine.

Today friends and family have arrived from England.
Yes, it's lovely to see them and over the next 48 hours my house
will be filled with those who come to mourn the loss of Luke and
to support us.
But, in truth, there's only one person I want to see, there's only
one I want to be here.

It's been almost a year - enough!
It's time you came home, Luke.

191

With all the love and all the tears, why can't this be reversed?
Why can't Luke not be dead?
What ceremony can I perform? What evil act can I commit to bring Luke back?

My sister reminded me today that "all the Hollywood in the world is not what made Luke special. It was Luke himself."
She is right.
But it's because Luke was special that he captured the hearts of Hollywood, as he did ours, from the lowliest to the most celebrated.
People old and young.
The beautiful and the ordinary.
Everyone feels they had a special relationship with him - not just since his life was cut so young - but in reading his phone I see that he had time for everyone - whoever they were.

It's this bond that now drives the good will forward, embodied in the phenomenon of lukelove, and I will harness it to continue his work and do good in this world.

I will never be as special to others as Luke,
but as his Mum I see people extending their hearts to me.
All this good will.
All this love.
We may not be able to bring him back, but we can turn it to good.

Whilst there is a breath in my body, Luke will never have died in vain.

lukelove is eternal.
Even if Luke was not.

APPRECIATION

It is 3.02 AM. A long planned pile of letters are now written, directly from my soul to those who have made me feel loved and of worth throughout the past 364 days.

Some have endured my depths of grief, others have given me mantras to live by.

There's so many more to write, but in truth, the cognac has taken me too far to finish any notes of worth.

But here I would be remiss, if I forget to write to myself, to my heart, to my brain, for taking me through thoughts I would never dare to consider. To my heart, so broken, which has continued to beat, though I've often begged it to stop, and to my body for staying steadfast through the abuse of sleep deprivation, insufficient nutrition and an assault of cigarettes and alcohol, so that I may live to consider another life beyond Luke, so that I may be a mother to George and a wife to Adam, a daughter, a sister, a friend and go forward and help others, either those who, like me, find themselves so deep in grief, or like Luke, lost in a tunnel of self destruction.

I miss Luke,
I miss me
neither of us will ever return.
Except
in a new form.

REMEMBRANCE

A glorious pillar-candle made by Adam.
Reformed from the remains of the scented Italian candles burned through each night since Luke died, now burns through this sad night and day, surrounded by votives for people to light in remembrance, atop a bed of moss and delicate flowers that evoke the spirit of Luke's cremation ceremony.

LET ME BELIEVE

The anniversary of Luke's departure has passed.
But the departure has not.

So suddenly and without goodbyes
he left.

So many regrets.
So much longing.
A magical boy.
A magnificent man, missed by so many.

All the lighting of all the candles in the world cannot change this.

My birthday approaches.
How can I celebrate my life?
When I don't even know it.

The pressure in my chest builds.
The loss pushes back on my breath.
I can soothe it for a moment, for a day, for an hour, but it is merely
a distraction before I return to my truth - the pain of a life without
Luke.

The shaping of a parent by their child (for parenthood is not
merely a shaping of a child) is for me the unexpected journey of
parenting. Now, a new chapter - the shaping of myself in the loss
of Luke and the grief of my surviving son.
The moments of overwhelming grief - not just mine - but that of
George and Adam - bring me to a new chapter in parental reshap-
ing.

The candle lighting is what I can do to honour Luke.
Not just a message to Luke that we love and honour him, but also to honour the loss that we feel collectively.

The writings that so many post on Luke's tribute page - the truth that grief is not something that one completes, but something one endures, something that one learns to live with - something that evolves and morphs - is now evident and tangible to me.

I remember Luke less and less in his bodily form and sometimes his presence in his post-life form is so real that I sense to grieve is to deny that.

Yes, I know how that sounds - that I do not accept that he is gone, but that he has merely left his body - but what harm does that do?

IF I'm imagining that Luke's spirit is all around me -
Why discount that?
Why break my spell?

If you think I am crazy - lock me up.
I'll still have Luke for company.

If that's the only way I can go forward; let me.
Acknowledge that, honour that.

If he is in spirit form all around
how much worse would that be, for him, that I deny it and leave him calling for me
unanswered, unacknowledged?

If I feel him, think of him, and it makes me smile
why deny me?

Why do people feel the need to break that spell?
Say they don't like the photo that he sent me, speak their thoughts on my reflection?
Why?

There's so much in this world that has not yet been discovered, explained. How can they be so cocksure?

I will stand by Luke, in death, as in life - I will enjoy his spiritual presence.
I will continue to have him guide me, keep me company.
I will not deny his excellent efforts to communicate.

The journey of a mother with a child in substance abuse leaves many in judgment - it's often a lonely road.

The journey of a mother in loss to substance abuse is the same.

My resolve was as strong as it was lonely during Luke's life.
It will remain strong in his death.
I am left changed, open to new possibilities.
I will honour that.
I will make a difference.
I will embrace the new Sheila and the new opportunities that come my way.

Is this denial?
Or is this a new skill?

Why would anyone care?
Why would you break that spell?

I love you Luke.

I love what you are.
I love all that I have learned about you since your death.
I love what I knew about you in life.
I will take your legacy.
I will take it forward.
In these times of judgment and conformism.
I will break the boundaries, as you did.
I will let you reshape me and
I will spread the lukelove.

If you are reading this
as a grieving mother
as a doubting therapist
as a person who works with substance abuse
as a substance abuser
in recovery
as a journalist

You will judge me.

For what I know.
For what you think I do not.
For what I did.
For what I didn't do
For what you think I don't understand.
For my addled mind in the grip of grief.

But before you do - think of love.
Think of common sense.
Think of possibilities beyond what awful reality we live with.

Luke loved people.
Old people.

Young people.
People flawed.
Rich,
poor,
influential,
famous - or not,
he could see you all.

Join together.
Support each other.
Luke was not the first boy to die.
Luke is not the last boy to die.

But what he brought to this world was that anything is possible.

I am taking that challenge to do the same.
To love myself.
To open my mind.
To change the world.
And the driving force -
is something he called
lukelove.

No one can ever take that away from me
and it's yours for the taking.

CREATING BEAUTY
IN LUKE'S NAME

Today is my birthday.
My last birthday was spent in a funeral home.
Then, catatonic, broken, in a trance, I found the strength to create beauty to honour Luke.

No casket, but a bed of green fragrant garlands to surround his beautiful, strong, proud form. Delicate blue flowers to be handed to the saddened souls that attended, to thread into the frame of greens, so in that purpose, they may find the courage to approach Luke's ice cold body and say their farewells.
Each memorial, first in London and last in Los Angeles, reflected this.
And now on the anniversary of his death - a work of green beauty and blue flowers, a bed for the votive candles people will light.

The drive to create beauty in Luke's name holds strong,
where my own resolve is fragile.
And so I will continue the theme on as long as I have a breath in my broken being.

I will create beauty where there is none.
I will bring light where there is dark.
And I will inspire courage in those who falter.
I will stay in truth
I will speak loud and proud

And maybe, just maybe...

A year on
and I can't stand it
all over again.

MEMORY

My memories are different to my physical reality, more a picture of my emotional reality.

At Luke's cremation, when I was called to speak - I am clear that I was halfway back in the pews, on my own and in the midst of picking something up from the floor.

When in fact I was at the front surrounded by loved ones.

My memory from the final sighting of Luke as he lay in the cremation oven, surrounded by flowers and garlands of green fragrant leaf - his hair, curly, golden, glorious and free.

I stood alone in front of the open oven, and as the door was closed, I remained a sole figure in front of the door, as if I was guarding Luke one final time, unable to know what to feel or how to feel, eyes fixed on the door.
When in fact, I am told, my sister stood behind me, holding me, hugging me all the while, of course she did, but this, I don't remember.

Do I only remember the emotional state of solitude?
Do I only remember my emotional truth?

MARRIAGE DIFFICULTIES
AFTER THE DEATH OF A CHILD

The statistics of marriage difficulties after the death of a child are very high.

It's past the one year mark and I am, for now, gathering strength.
Adam is, tonight, seemingly losing his.
As we twist and turn through our pathway of grief, as now, there are moments of parting of empathy and kindness.
We are struggling.
Adam is angry tonight and appears to be irritated by me.
Snatching, carping.
This is a pattern of old and I fear its return bodes badly for our marriage because if I am to find a way forward in my loss of Luke, Adam's anger expressed towards me will be a further burden that I cannot bear.

As if now he feels I can take it.
So why have I swum so, towards the surface?
On that count I was better in the grief's depths of despair.
Is it that from those depths I could not feel that anger?
Or is it that he has come to the end of his tether?
He's been so amazing, is he just out of strength?
Can I help him?
Can I take it?
Should I duck back into my black cloud of despair to dodge it?
Or is it just the toll of this loss crashing down on us - finally?
Intimacy is hard.
Sex out of the question for me.
The trauma of the last time, the reminder of that last night of happiness with Luke so present in our lovemaking as he left this

world.

I would seek solitude over this.

But is it my time to help him? As he has helped me?

Can I find that strength in my fragile resolve?

Or is it a step too far?

I feel that I have done that so much in this marriage.

Am I done trying to fix it?

Or is this why marriages often don't make it through the loss of a child?

And is it different when that child is killed by drugs?

Are we angry at each other?

Do we feel the other could have done more?

Is the honeymoon period over?

Is my marriage to be part of the roadkill?

Or does he just not love the person I have become?

Or are we just both exhausted?

FAMILIAR RITUALS

So this was the date of Luke's London memorial.

Stage two of the farewell tour, the ashes placed on a table before the altar at the Swedish church.

Not just any table, but a table built by a dear friend and swathed in moss and lingon leaves gathered lovingly by my cousin and her grandchildren from the beds of the Swedish forest, where Luke first rode his beloved pony, Netti.

Atop, a photograph of Luke laid out in Boston. A reminder, a gesture to those who needed to know why we were there - Luke was dead.

I pledged that although we had let his body go in Boston, this was the day that I would let his soul go.

Transfixed on the painting above the altar, before which my marriage was blessed and Luke and George were christened, I begged Jesus to take care of him.

Am I religious?

Who knows?

But I was taking no chances with my sweet Luke's soul.

The hordes of people processed in to lay flowers by his ashes, by the light of the solitary candle from the Farmaceutica de Santa Maria Novella in Florence where he had stood as a tiny child, that became the symbol from my Mother's eulogy, for 'leaving a light on for Luke', who, as a child, had been so scared of the dark.

A symbol that lasts 'til now as we light a candle each night by his ashes at our bedside, which burns through the dark of each night.

Does it make me feel better?

Better than what?

In the absence of Luke, these are the rituals of remembrance and contemplation that we perform.
To mark our loss,
To pay homage to Luke,
To outwardly display that we are changed in his loss.

A sign to Luke that we miss him,
that we think of him,
a ritual that we invite his grieving friends to perform, should they wish, and so to
honour our recognition of their loss of our son.
We set the tone for others.
For this grief is not a test which we are to complete.
This is a loss we endure for all eternity.

A gradual acceptance.
A gradual stepping forward without him on uncertain ground.

Am I in a better place than I was a year ago?
Yes, I drive.
Yes, I speak.
Yes, I complete some daily functions.
Yes, I'm still alive.

But in truth, it is more that I have become familiar with feeling this unbearable loss.

How shit is that?

A YEAR ON

I have moved through many mindsets, many scenarios.

A year on from Luke's death, there are still so many questions unanswered.
It is clear to me that in order to fully close the loop of my trauma I will have to know exactly what happened that night.
It does not suffice to just take the medical examiner's report and all that I have found out myself about his drug use from his phone, from his friends.

It's not revenge or judgment that I seek, merely the truth.
However ugly.
The truth.
The full picture.
The unfiltered truth.

So, what are the questions that I need answered?
What answers will allow me to close the trauma loop?

The circumstances and events.
The method Luke used to take the deadly dose.
Luke's state of mind before and after.
Who was there?
The final twists that led to his death to heroin.

The dark and consuming black hole of that night, that I fear, if I do not fill it in with truth, will consume me forever.
I will never be able to move forward, to rest, to close the loop and move forward, in acceptance, in fact.

And how do I get those answers?

The one person who may or may not be able to enlighten me -
too scared,
too guilty,
too self-preserving,
or too fuck knows what
to tell me.
It's all about him.

How fucked up is that?

THE CURSE OF
CHRISTMAS

How to escape our reality and find a safe place to be with distractions from our reality at a time when families gather and ours is broken?

Feeling our burden on ourselves and upon others.
There's no natural place to be.
The effort to find somewhere to go is heavy.
The death of a child is forever, and not just for Christmas.
But Christmas is an issue for us.
The reminder, the empty chair, for us, so strong, as others go back to their lives.
As they should.
But we are left in intolerable pain.
Paralysis in our loss, not always insurmountable, but heightened by holidays.
I wish I had more optimism to impart.

FUCK DRUGS.

CLOSURE

Searching for a way to draw a close to this journal.

But there's no meaningful way.
So much still unanswered.
The questions, the seeking did not come to an end a year on.
The 'firsts' have all passed.
The celebrations of Luke's life, the memorials, all passed.

There's no finale.
No big enlightenment.
This was not a test, a task to complete where the reward of Luke's return is bestowed.
This will be so forever.

I would have liked to offer a cure to how I feel.
I would have liked to offer an answer to prevent this from happening to anyone else.
But I have not found it.

As I sit here, back outside on the deck, cigarette in hand, as I did so many nights with my journal and before his death, with Luke - yes, I am walking, talking, driving.
I can perform the tasks of everyday life, albeit in a new form. In a new version of myself.

My friends and family and Luke's friends all bring love and support that are a huge part of how I made it to this point.
They just keep showing up.
It's what the grief books advise, and it has worked - even when I didn't feel it.

And I certainly don't have a true recollection of all that they have done for us.

But what prevails is their bravery to face, support, and love me on this dreadful journey, despite the horrors that it must surely bring to their hearts.
No stigma.

I will always miss Luke.
I see now that it's a loss that is forever.
As indelibly marked on my skin as in my heart;
The thing that is so hard to bear;
The loss of my firstborn son, Luke.
A brilliant and charming, magical boy.
A light that burned so bright for 23 years, 3 months, and 24 days, leaving us too soon;
Stunned, baffled, and broken -

but always with lukelove.

Made in the USA
Las Vegas, NV
03 February 2024

85217546R00126